The Institute of Chartered Accountants in England and Wales

ASSURANCE

Professional Stage Knowledge Level

For exams in 2013

Question Bank

www.icaew.com

Assurance
The Institute of Chartered Accountants in England and Wales Professional Stage

ISBN: 978-0-85760-449-1

Previous ISBN: 978-0-85760-219-0

First edition 2007
Sixth edition 2012

British Library Cataloguing-in-Publication Data
A catalogue record for this book is available from the British Library

Printed in the United Kingdom by Polestar Wheatons

Polestar Wheatons
Hennock Road
Marsh Barton
Exeter
EX2 8RP

Your learning materials are printed on paper sourced from traceable, sustainable sources.

Contents

Title		Page	
		Questions	Answers
1.	Concept of and need for assurance	3	101
2.	Process of assurance: obtaining an engagement	9	103
3.	Process of assurance: planning the assignment	13	105
4.	Process of assurance: evidence and reporting	21	109
5.	Introduction to internal control	25	111
6.	Revenue system	35	115
7.	Purchases system	39	117
8.	Employee costs	43	119
9.	Internal audit	47	121
10.	Documentation	51	123
11.	Evidence and sampling	55	125
12.	Written representations	63	129
13.	Substantive procedures – key financial statement figures	67	131
14.	Codes of professional ethics	79	135
15.	Integrity, objectivity and independence	83	137
16.	Confidentiality	95	141

Question Bank

Your exam will consist of 50 questions with equal marks, together adding up to 100 marks. You should complete them all.

The questions are of the following types:

- **Multiple choice** – select 1 from 4 options A, B, C or D (see Chapter 1 Q3)

- **Multiple response** – select 2 or more responses from 4 or more options (see Chapter 1 Q1)

- **Multi-part multiple choice** – select 1 from 2, 3 or 4 options, for two or more question parts (see Chapter 1 Q7)

Chapter 1: Concept of and need for assurance

1   Which THREE of the following are key elements of a general assurance engagement?

   A   A user

   B   A subject matter

   C   Suitable criteria

   D   An assurance file   LO 1a

2   Which THREE of the following describe aspects of the expectations gap with respect to the external audit?

   A   Users do not understand the meaning of the audit opinion

   B   Users are not aware of the limitations of the audit process

   C   Users do not appreciate that reasonable assurance is a low level of assurance

   D   Users do not understand what the audit process involves   LO 1e

3   Which of the following qualifications is required for individuals working on audits in the UK?

   A   University degree

   B   Professional qualification

   C   Membership of a recognised supervisory body

   D   Employment by a firm controlled by qualified persons   LO 1f

4   Which TWO of the following are limitations of the provision of assurance?

   A   Assurance work is carried out by people independent of the entity

   B   Sampling is used in assurance work

   C   Client systems have inherent limitations

   D   Unqualified staff may be used on assurance engagements   LO 1e

5   In any assurance engagement there are three parties involved: the responsible party, the practitioner and the user.

    In respect of given subject matter state which party

    Determines the suitable criteria

    A   User

    B   Practitioner

    C   Responsible party

    Provides an opinion on whether the subject matter complies with the criteria

    D   User

    E   Practitioner

    F   Responsible party   LO 1c

6   Which of the following statements best describes the evidence obtained and the opinion given in a reasonable assurance engagement?

    A   Sufficient appropriate evidence and a negative opinion

    B   Sufficient appropriate evidence and a positive opinion

    C   A lower level of evidence and a negative opinion

    D   A lower level of evidence and a positive opinion   LO 1h

7   For each of the following statements select whether they are true or false.

    A statutory audit gives reasonable assurance that the financial statements give a true and fair view

    A   True

    B   False

    A negative assurance conclusion gives a limited level of assurance

    C   True

    D   False

    Reasonable assurance is absolute assurance of the correctness of the subject matter

    E   True

    F   False   LO 1d

8   Jones & Co is the external auditor of Blue plc, a listed company. The directors of Blue plc have requested that Jones & Co carry out a review engagement assessing the effectiveness of its corporate governance policies against the UK Corporate Governance Code.

For the above review engagement, select which part of the engagement description constitutes the subject matter, which describes the suitable criteria and which party is the responsible party.

The subject matter

A   Blue plc's corporate governance policies

B   The UK Corporate Governance Code

The suitable criteria

C   Blue plc's corporate governance policies

D   The UK Corporate Governance Code

The responsible party

E   Jones & Co

F   The directors of Blue plc   LO 1a/c

9   For each of the following statements select whether they are true or false in respect of suitable criteria used in an assurance engagement.

The criteria for all assurance engagements will be the same

A   True

B   False

Suitable criteria can only be identified for assurance engagements relating to financial statements

C   True

D   False

Relevant criteria for assurance engagements relating to financial statements are likely to be accounting standards

E   True

F   False   LO 1d

10 There are two types of assurance engagement: reasonable assurance engagements and limited assurance engagements. There are also two types of assurance conclusion: positive and negative.

For each type of assurance engagement select the appropriate conclusion given.

Reasonable assurance

A   Positive

B   Negative

Limited assurance

C   Positive

D   Negative   LO 1d

11   For each of the following statements relating to the provisions of the Companies Act 2006, select whether they are true or false

An individual or firm is eligible for appointment as statutory auditor if the individual or firm is a member of a recognised supervisory body and is eligible for appointment under the rules of that body

A   True

B   False

A person may not act as a statutory auditor if that person is an officer or employee of the audit client

C   True

D   False   LO 1f

12   Which of the following best describes the concept of assurance?

Assurance refers to

A   An assurance firm's high level of satisfaction as to the reliability of an assertion being made by one party for the use of another party

B   An assurance firm's satisfaction as to the reliability of an assertion being made by one party for the use of another party

C   A user's satisfaction as to the reliability of an assertion being made by another party

D   An assurance firm's limited level of satisfaction as to the reliability of an assertion being made by one party for the use of another party   LO 1a

13   Which of the following is NOT a benefit of an assurance report on financial information?

An assurance report

A   Enhances the credibility of the information being reported upon

B   Reduces the risk of management bias in the information being reported upon

C   Attests to the correctness of the information being reported upon

D   Draws the attention of the user to deficiencies in the information being reported upon   LO 1b

14   In any assurance engagement there are three parties involved: the responsible party, the practitioner and the user.

In respect of given subject matter state which party

Prepares the subject matter

A   Responsible party

B   Practitioner

C   User

Gathers evidence on the subject matter

D   Responsible party

E   Practitioner

F   User   LO 1c

15 The following is an extract from an independent accountant's unmodified report on a profit forecast:

'Based on our examination of the evidence supporting the assumptions, nothing has come to our attention which causes us to believe that these assumptions do not provide a reasonable basis for the forecast.'

Which of the following BEST describes the type of assurance provided by this statement?

A   Positive assurance expressed negatively

B   Negative assurance expressed positively

C   High level of assurance expressed negatively

D   Limited level of assurance expressed negatively   LO 1d

16 In the context of a statutory audit which THREE of the following are examples of the expectation gap?

The belief that

A   The auditor's report certifies the financial statements as correct

B   The auditor's principal duty is to detect fraud

C   The auditor is employed by the directors

D   The auditor checks all transactions   LO 1e

17 The level of assurance given by an assurance engagement will depend on the type of engagement.

For each of the following examples select what level of assurance you would expect to be given.

Statutory audit

A   Absolute

B   Reasonable

Review of financial information

C   Reasonable

D   Limited

Report on a business plan

E   Reasonable

F   Limited   LO 1d

Assurance: Question Bank

Chapter 2: Process of assurance: obtaining an engagement

1   Which TWO of the following are auditors ALWAYS required to do on being invited to accept an audit engagement?

   A   Ensure they are professionally qualified to act

   B   Ensure they have adequate existing resources to carry out the audit

   C   Obtain references for key personnel within the entity to be audited

   D   Communicate with the existing auditors to discover any reasons they should not accept appointment

   LO 1f

2   Which TWO of the following might indicate that an assurance client could be higher than normal inherent or control risk?

   A   Poor recent performance

   B   Strong internal controls

   C   Unusual transactions

   D   The existence of an internal audit department

   LO 1f

3   Claret & Co, an assurance firm, has the following two clients among its client portfolio. For each client, select whether inherent risk is high or low.

   Tulip Ltd is planning to list on the local stock exchange within the next two years

   A   High risk

   B   Low risk

   Dhalia Ltd is currently facing financial difficulties and is seeking alternative forms of finance

   C   High risk

   D   Low risk

   LO 1f

4   Which of the following is NOT a benefit of an engagement letter in respect of assurance services?

   A   Clearly defines the extent of the assurance provider's responsibilities

   B   Provides written confirmation of the acceptance of the engagement

   C   Confirms the scope of the engagement

   D   Certifies the assurance provider's opinion

   LO 1f

5   For each of the following factors at a prospective client select whether that factor indicates that that client is high risk or low risk.

Company has prudent accounting policies

A   High risk

B   Low risk

Company carries out unusual transactions

C   High risk

D   Low risk

Company currently has no finance director

E   High risk

F   Low risk   LO 1f

6   Auditors issue various documents during the process of obtaining clients. For each of the following, select the type of document it would be included in.

Clarification of the terms of the engagement

A   Tender proposal

B   Initial communication

C   Letter of engagement

Request for relevant information pertaining to acceptance of the engagement

D   Tender proposal

E   Initial communication

F   Letter of engagement   LO 1f

7   Which THREE of the following procedures should be carried out after the audit firm has decided to accept appointment as auditor?

A   Ensure that the outgoing auditors' removal /resignation has been properly conducted

B   Ensure that a resolution has been passed at the general meeting to appoint the new auditors

C   Perform checks to ensure that there are no legal or ethical reasons why the new audit firm cannot act as auditor

D   Submit a letter of engagement to the directors   LO 1f

8   For each of the following statements select whether they are true or false in respect of the audit engagement letter.

The engagement letter should be sent before acceptance of appointment

A   True

B   False

The engagement letter should be sent after the appointment of the auditor but before the commencement of the audit

C   True

D   False

The engagement letter should be sent after the commencement of the audit but before the signing of the auditor's report

E   True

F   False

An engagement letter should be sent to all new clients

G   True

H   False   LO 1f

9   Which ONE of the following correctly describes the period for which client identification documents must be kept under money laundering regulations?

A   For a minimum of five years and until five years have elapsed since the relationship with the client has ceased

B   For a minimum of seven years and until seven years have elapsed since the relationship with the client has ceased

C   For a minimum of five years and until seven years have elapsed since the relationship with the client has ceased

D   For a minimum of seven years and until five years have elapsed since the relationship with the client has ceased   LO 1f

10 Which TWO of the following MUST be included in the engagement letter?

A   The responsibilities of the auditor

B   Arrangements regarding the planning and performance of the audit

C   The form of any reports

D   Basis on which fees are computed   LO 1f

11 Which THREE of the following are purposes of a letter of engagement?

A   Setting out the form of any report to be issued

B   Providing constructive suggestions to management concerning improvements in internal control

C   Documenting and confirming acceptance of the appointment

D   Narrowing the expectations gap

E   Providing evidence on matters where other evidence is not expected to exist   LO 1f

12   Which of the following best describes professional scepticism?

The assurance provider should

A   Not believe anything that management tells him

B   Not believe anything that management tells him, without obtaining supporting evidence

C   Apply a questioning mind to the information and evidence he obtains

D   Always assume the worst outcome in cases of uncertainty   LO 1g

Chapter 3: Process of assurance: planning the assignment

1   Which THREE of the following are objectives of audit planning?

    A   To determine the scope of the engagement

    B   To ensure appropriate attention is devoted to the important areas of the audit

    C   To identify potential problems and resolve them on a timely basis

    D   To assign work to members of the audit team   LO 1f

2   With respect to ISA 315, which THREE of the following procedures shall be used in understanding the entity and its environment?

    A   Inquiries of management and others within the entity

    B   Inquiries of third parties

    C   Analytical procedures

    D   Observation and inspection   LO 1f

3   Which THREE of the following constitute analytical procedures?

    A   Consideration of comparable information for prior periods

    B   Consideration of relationships between elements of financial information that are expected to conform to a predicted pattern

    C   Consideration of whether a balance has been calculated correctly

    D   Consideration of similar industry information   LO 1f

4   Which of the following does setting a preliminary materiality threshold NOT help auditors to decide?

    A   What audit staff to assign to the audit

    B   How many items to examine

    C   Whether to use sampling

    D   What level of error is likely to lead to the auditor not being able to give an unqualified opinion   LO 1f

5   Which THREE of the following would normally be included in the overall audit strategy?

    A   Details of economic factors and industry conditions

    B   The results of initial analytical procedures

    C   Confirmation of management's responsibility for the financial statements

    D   Identification of specific audit risks   LO 1f

6   In each of the following cases, select whether inherent risk is higher or lower than normal.

The company operates a profit-related pay scheme

A   Inherent risk higher than normal

B   Inherent risk lower than normal

The business is of the company is cash-based

C   Inherent risk higher than normal

D   Inherent risk lower than normal

Financial statements contain balances with straightforward financial accounting requirements

E   Inherent risk higher than normal

F   Inherent risk lower than normal   LO 1f

7   For each of the following statements select whether they are true or false in respect of the concept of materiality.

Materiality may depend on the size of the error in the context of its omission or misstatement

A   True

B   False

Materiality should be considered when planning audit procedures and when evaluating discovered misstatements

C   True

D   False

Materiality is always expressed as a proportion of profits

E   True

F   False   LO 1f

8   Audit risk can be split into three components: inherent risk, control risk and detection risk.

For each of the following examples, select the type of risk illustrated.

The organisation is seeking to raise finance for a new venture

A   Inherent

B   Control

C   Detection

The organisation has a number of estimates in its financial statements

D   Inherent

E   Control

F   Detection   LO 1f

9   Audit risk can be split into three components: inherent risk, control risk and detection risk.

For each of the following examples, select the type of risk illustrated.

The organisation has a high turnover of staff in the accounts department

A   Inherent

B   Control

C   Detection

The auditor will be using samples in testing

D   Inherent

E   Control

F   Detection   LO 1f

10   Adam has been given the following draft figures for Imperious Ltd for the year ended 30 June 20X7 to analyse. Materiality has been set at £35,000 and the finance director has told Adam in a planning meeting that there have been few changes in the year. Budgets were set at 20X6 levels and there have been no major movements in non-current assets.

	20X7	20X6
	£	£
Revenue	3,497,284	3,487,286
Cost of sales	1,867,294	2,008,967
Salaries	467,900	420,975
Repairs and renewals	3,645	3,800
Depreciation	4,598	4,365
Advertising	37,945	37,283

For each item identified below, state whether it warrants further testing to analytical procedures or not.

Cost of sales

A   Warrants further testing

B   No further testing required

Repairs and renewals

C   Warrants further testing

D   No further testing required

Advertising

E   Warrants further testing

F   No further testing required   LO 1f

11 Which TWO of the following would be used in understanding the entity in accordance with ISA 315?

A   Industry, regulatory and other external factors

B   A preliminary review of internal controls

C   The results of tests of details

D   The results of a review of events after the date of the financial statements   LO 1f

12 Which of the following is normally designed to detect possible material monetary errors in the figures in financial statements?

A   Test of control

B   Walk-through test

C   Analytical procedure

D   Observation of a procedure   LO 3f

13 For each of the following statements select whether they are true or false in respect of the concept of materiality.

Materiality should be calculated at the planning stage of all audits

A   True

B   False

Once established, the materiality level initially set cannot be revised during the course of the audit

C   True

D   False

Materiality will influence the audit opinion given

E   True

F   False   LO 1f

14 Audit risk can be split into three components: inherent risk, control risk and detection risk

For each of the following examples, select the type of risk illustrated.

Senior management regularly override the system of controls

A   Inherent

B   Control

C   Detection

Directors' pay is related to company profitability

D   Inherent

E   Control

F   Detection   LO 1f

15 Which THREE of the following would increase inherent risk?

  A Sample sizes have been calculated incorrectly by the auditor and are too small

  B A significant number of balances are based on estimates

  C The financial statements include complex transactions

  D Audit staff are inexperienced

  E The company is seeking to raise finance   LO 1f

16 As part of his overall risk assessment an auditor has concluded that detection risk must be low. For
   each of the following select the appropriate consequence of this.

  Materiality

  A Higher

  B Lower

  Sample sizes

  C Bigger

  D Smaller   LO 1f

17 For each of the following situations select the MOST appropriate approach which should be used
   by the assurance firm in the given circumstance.

   The audit of a new client, recently started up, with few employees in its accounting department

  A Tests of control only

  B Substantive procedures only

  C A mix of tests of control and substantive procedures

   The audit of a long-standing client with a sophisticated IT system and an internal audit department

  D Tests of control only

  E Substantive procedures only

  F A mix of tests of control and substantive procedures   LO 3f

18 As part of your analytical procedures on the financial statements of Dreamy Desserts Ltd you have
   identified that the gross profit margin has fallen from 27% to 24%.

   Which TWO of the following could be a valid explanation for this decrease?

  A Unusually high sales at the end of the year resulted in lower levels of closing inventory as
     compared to the previous year

  B Increased competition resulted in sales prices being cut

  C A bank overdraft resulted in a higher interest expense than in previous years

  D There was a significant change in the mix of products sold   LO 1f/3g

19 In each of the following cases, select whether inherent risk is higher or lower than normal.

The company has recently listed on the local stock exchange with high profit expectations from analysts

A   Inherent risk higher than normal

B   Inherent risk lower than normal

Inventory is the largest balance on the balance sheet

C   Inherent risk higher than normal

D   Inherent risk lower than normal

The company operates in a slow-moving, stable industry

E   Inherent risk higher than normal

F   Inherent risk lower than normal   LO 1f

20 For each of the following statements select whether they are true or false in respect of the concept of materiality.

Materiality depends only on the monetary amount of an item

A   True

B   False

Materiality may depend on either the nature of an item or its monetary amount

C   True

D   False

Materiality is a matter of professional judgment

E   True

F   False   LO 1f

21 Audit risk can be split into three components: inherent risk, control risk and detection risk.

For each of the following examples select the type of risk illustrated.

The organisation has few employees in its accounting department

A   Inherent

B   Control

C   Detection

The organisation operates in a fast-moving, high-tech environment

D   Inherent

E   Control

F   Detection   LO 1f

22 Which one or more of the following options are signs of overtrading?

    A   Inventory decreasing

    B   Cash decreasing

    C   Payables decreasing

    D   Receivables increasing   LO 1f

23 Deteriora Ltd's quick ratio has fallen from 1.9:1 to 1.6:1. Which of the following might help to
    explain this decline?

    A   The allowance for receivables has been reduced

    B   Credit control has been poor

    C   The entity has purchased a property for cash

    D   Inventory levels have fallen   LO 1f

24 An electrical store and a cake shop have the same mark-up on cost. However, the gross profit
    margin of the electrical store is significantly higher than that of the cake shop.

    Which of the following is a possible reason for this?

    A   The cake shop's revenue is increasing, while that of the electrical shop is decreasing

    B   The cake shop has a higher level of wastage of inventory than the electrical store

    C   The electrical shop takes advantage of trade discounts for bulk buying

    D   The cake shop has a higher turnover of inventory than the electrical store   LO 1f

25 Thatch plc's current ratio this year is 1.33:1 compared with 1.25:1 last year. Which of the following
    would be possible explanations of this?

    A   Thatch paid its payables earlier than usual out of a bank overdraft

    B   Thatch made an unusually large sale immediately prior to the year end

    C   Thatch made an unusually large purchase of goods for cash immediately prior to the year end,
         and these goods remain in inventory

    D   Thatch paid its payables earlier than usual out of a positive cash balance   LO 1f

Assurance: Question Bank

Chapter 4: Process of assurance: evidence and reporting

1   Which of the following is NOT a test that could be used by assurance providers to provide evidence relating to a balance in the financial statements?

    A   Walk-through test

    B   Test of control

    C   Test of detail

    D   Analytical procedure

                                                    LO 3b

2   Which TWO of the following are valid comments about the quality of assurance evidence?

    A   Evidence from external sources is more reliable than evidence obtained from the entity's records

    B   Evidence from internal sources is more reliable when related internal controls operate effectively

    C   Evidence from internal sources is more reliable than evidence created by the assurance provider

    D   Photocopies are more reliable than facsimiles

                                                    LO 3e

3   Which THREE of the following are assertions used by the auditor about classes of transactions?

    A   Occurrence

    B   Existence

    C   Completeness

    D   Cut-off

    E   Rights and obligations

                                                    LO 3f

4   Which THREE of the following statements are valid?

    A   Positive assurance will be given on a statutory audit assignment

    B   Positive assurance requires more rigorous work to be undertaken than negative assurance does

    C   Positive assurance will be given on a review assignment

    D   Negative assurance is assurance given in the absence of any indications to the contrary

                                                    LO 1d

5   Which TWO of the following describe manifestations of the expectations gap?

    A   Users blaming the auditors for a fraud discovered in a company subsequent to an audit

    B   Users discovering that the directors refuse to cooperate in providing the auditor with the evidence he requests

    C   Shareholders approving the appointment of the auditor at an annual general meeting

    D   Users relying on the audited financial statements as a fair valuation of the company

LO 1e

6   The level of assurance given by an assurance engagement will depend on the type of engagement.

For each of the following examples, select what level of assurance you would expect to be given.

Statutory audit

    A   Absolute

    B   Reasonable

    C   Limited

Report on prospective financial information

    D   Absolute

    E   Reasonable

    F   Limited

Report on review of interim financial information

    G   Absolute

    H   Reasonable

    I   Limited

LO 1d

7   For each of the following situations select the most appropriate approach which should be used by the assurance firm in the given circumstances.

The audit of a client where controls have been assessed as deficient

    A   Tests of controls only

    B   Substantive procedures only

    C   A mix of tests of controls and substantive procedures

The audit of a client where controls have been assessed as strong

    D   Tests of controls only

    E   Substantive procedures only

    F   A mix of tests of controls and substantive procedures

LO 3f

8   The following are types of test that might be carried out by an assurance provider. For each example select the financial statement assertion that is being tested.

    Review of the financial statements using a Companies Act checklist

    A   Existence

    B   Completeness

    C   Classification

    Tracing non-current assets which have been observed in use back to the non-current asset register

    D   Existence

    E   Completeness

    F   Classification   LO 3d

9   Which TWO of the following are assertions used by the auditor about account balances at the period end?

    A   Existence

    B   Accuracy

    C   Cut-off

    D   Completeness   LO 3f

10 Which TWO of the following are assertions used by the auditor about presentation and disclosure?

    A   Cut-off

    B   Allocation

    C   Completeness

    D   Accuracy   LO 3f

11 For each of the following statements select whether they are true or false in respect of substantive procedures.

    The auditor must carry out substantive procedures on all material items

    A   True

    B   False

    The auditor only carries out substantive procedures if the results of tests of controls are inconclusive

    C   True

    D   False

    Substantive procedures include both analytical procedures and tests of details

    E   True

    F   False   LO 3d

12   Two types of procedures used in gathering evidence are tests of controls and substantive procedures.

For each of the following examples select the type of procedure illustrated.

Observation of opening the post

A   Test of control

B   Substantive procedure

Calculation of the gross profit margin and comparison with that of the previous accounting period

C   Test of control

D   Substantive procedure

Reviewing invoices paid for evidence of authorisation

E   Test of control

F   Substantive procedure   LO 3b

13   An audit report prepared in accordance with ISA 700 (UK & Ireland) *The auditor's report on financial statements* expresses an opinion on a number of matters. Some of these matters are required by the Companies Act 2006 to be reported on by exception only.

Which TWO of the following are reported on by exception only?

A   The financial statements have been prepared in accordance with the requirements of the Companies Act 2006

B   Adequate accounting records have been kept

C   Directors' remuneration has been disclosed correctly

D   Information in the directors' report is consistent with the financial statements   LO 1f

Chapter 5: Introduction to internal control

1 ISA 315 states that an internal control system in an organisation consists of five components: the control environment, the entity's risk assessment process, the information system, control activities and monitoring of controls.

For each of the following examples, select the component which it illustrates.

The process of preparing the financial statements

A   Control environment

B   Information system

C   Control activities

Locking the inventory storeroom

D   Control environment

E   Information system

F   Control activities   LO 2d

2 In each of the following three cases, select whether control risk is higher or lower than normal.

The company has an established and well-resourced internal audit function.

A   Control risk is higher than normal

B   Control risk is lower than normal

The company has a history of reviewing financial performance on a regular basis at board level

C   Control risk is higher than normal

D   Control risk is lower than normal

Purchase invoices are not authorised prior to payment

E   Control risk is higher than normal

F   Control risk is lower than normal   LO 2b

3 Which THREE of the following statements about audit committees are correct?

A   At least 50% of the members of an audit committee must be non-executive directors

B   Listed companies are required to have an audit committee

C   Audit committees are considered to be good practice for all large companies

D   If a company has an internal audit function, the chief internal auditor should sit on the audit committee

E   Audit committees are an important aspect of a company's control environment   LO 2d

4   According to ISA 315 which THREE of the following are aspects of an entity's control environment?

    A   The attitude of the directors to internal controls

    B   The attitude of staff to internal controls

    C   The awareness of internal control issues in the company

    D   The actions of senior management in relation to internal controls   LO 2d

5   For each of the following internal controls, which is the principal limitation?

    The preparation of a bank reconciliation

    A   Human error

    B   Collusion

    Segregation of duties in a sales system

    C   Human error

    D   Collusion   LO 2f

6   Which of the following is not part of an entity's risk assessment process?

    A   Identify relevant business risks

    B   Estimate the impact of risks

    C   Assess the likelihood of occurrence

    D   Decide upon actions to manage the risks

    E   Report the process to the auditors   LO 2b

7   For each of the following statements, select whether they are true or false in respect of the information system in a company.

    The information system comprises only the IT system in a company

    A   True

    B   False

    The information system includes the process of preparing the financial statements, such as the production of journals

    C   True

    D   False   LO 2b

8   The following are examples of internal controls which operate at Badweather plc.

For each example, select the type of control activity which it illustrates.

The financial controller counts petty cash on a monthly basis

A   Authorisation

B   Information processing

C   Physical control

There are two keys to the locked finance department safe: one held by the finance director and the other by the managing director

D   Authorisation

E   Information processing

F   Physical control   LO 2e

9   The following are examples of internal controls which operate at Castle Ltd.

For each example, select the type of control activity which it illustrates.

The financial controller reconciles the receivables ledger to the receivables ledger control account monthly

A   Performance review

B   Information processing

C   Segregation of duties

The receivables ledger clerk posts invoices to the receivables ledger. The cash book clerk posts cash receipts to the receivables ledger

D   Performance review

E   Information processing

F   Segregation of duties   LO 2e

10   The following are examples of computer controls which operate at Goody plc.

For each example, select the type of computer control which it illustrates.

Storing extra copies of programs and data files off-site

A   General

B   Application

Programmes to check data fields on input transactions

C   General

D   Application

Manual checks to ensure that input data was authorised

E   General

F   Application   LO 2e

11 Which of the following would be the simplest way of recording a straightforward system not subject to a great deal of change annually?

A   Flowchart

B   Narrative notes

C   Questionnaire

D   Family tree   LO 2i

12 Which THREE of the following would be the best sources of information about a company's systems?

A   The company's procedures manual

B   The internal audit function's system notes

C   The prior year audit file

D   Inquiries made of company staff

E   The company's website   LO 2i

13 Most entities make use of IT systems for financial reporting and operational purposes. Controls operating in an IT environment can be split into general controls and application controls.

Which of the following is an application control?

A   Training staff in new IT procedures

B   Taking back-up copies of programs

C   Maintenance agreements over IT equipment

D   Cyclical reviews of all master files   LO 2e

14 Which TWO of the following represent inherent limitations of a system of internal controls?

A   Lack of controls over the purchases system

B   Lack of understanding of the purposes of controls

C   Lack of staff to ensure segregation of duties

D   The possibility that staff members will collude in fraud   LO 2f

15 Which TWO of the following are authorisation control activities?

A   A bank reconciliation signed by the finance director

B   A cheque payment run approved by the finance director

C   An appraisal of the sales ledger clerk by the finance director

D   A trial balance compiled by the finance director   LO 2e

16   With regards to internal control systems in small entities, select whether each of the following statements is true or false.

Smaller companies are more likely to be successful in the implementation of segregation of duties controls

A   True

B   False

Management override is more likely to take place in smaller companies

C   True

D   False   LO 2f

17   ISA 315 states that an internal control system in an organisation consists of five components: the control environment, the entity's risk assessment process, the information system, control activities and monitoring of controls.

For each of the following examples select the component which it illustrates.

Training programme for all staff

A   Control environment

B   Control activity

C   Monitoring of controls

Review of actual performance against budget

D   Control environment

E   Control activity

F   Monitoring of controls   LO 2d

18   For each of the following statements select whether they are true or false in respect of the limitations of a system of internal control.

The cost of implementing controls may be more expensive than the cost of any potential risk arising

A   True

B   False

The effectiveness of many controls rely on the integrity of those applying them

C   True

D   False

Internal controls are only applied to material items

E   True

F   False

Standard controls may not be designed to deal with unusual transactions

G   True

H   False   LO 2f

19   For each of the following statements select whether they are true or false in respect of business risk.

Business risk is the risk inherent to the company in its operations

A   True

B   False

Business risk is of no relevance to the auditor. The auditor is only concerned with audit risk

C   True

D   False

Management are responsible for identifying and controlling business risks

E   True

F   False   LO 2b

20   One of the five elements of internal control is monitoring of controls.

Which TWO of the following are activities which would be used to monitor controls?

A   Management's review of whether bank reconciliations are being prepared on a timely basis

B   Internal auditors' evaluation of whether the sales team are following company policy regarding customer discounts

C   Authorisation of purchase invoices before they are paid

D   Authorisation of purchase orders by the department manager   LO 2e

21   The following are examples of internal controls which operate at Elm plc.

For each example, select the type of control activity which it illustrates.

The financial controller reconciles the payables ledger to the payables ledger control account on a monthly basis

A   Performance review

B   Information processing

The payables ledger clerk posts invoices to the payables ledger. The cash book clerk posts cash receipts to the payables ledger

C   Segregation of duties

D   Performance review   LO 2e

22   The following are examples of computer controls which operate in the payroll system at Dobson Ltd.

For each example, select the type of computer control which it illustrates.

Password protection limiting access to data

A   General

B   Application

Range checks on payroll processing

C   General

D   Application

Manual checks to ensure that timesheets are authorised before details are processed

E   General

F   Application   LO 2e

23   Which of the following is NOT a general control?

A   Disaster recovery procedures

B   Back-up copies of programs stored at an alternative safe location

C   Procedures for resubmission of rejected data

D   Staff training in the use of new/revised programs   LO 2e

24   Peach plc is a large organisation with a complex accounting and information system. Critical to an understanding of the system are the reporting lines and relationships between different departments.

In this situation which of the following methods is most likely to be used by the auditor to record the system of document flow?

A   Narrative notes

B   Flowcharts

C   Questionnaires

D   Organisational charts   LO 2i

25   In each of the following three cases, select whether control risk is higher or lower than normal.

The payables ledger is not regularly reconciled to the payables ledger control account

A   Control risk is higher than normal

B   Control risk is lower than normal

Management often override internal controls

C   Control risk is higher than normal

D   Control risk is lower than normal

Entry to the inventory storeroom is only for authorised personnel

E   Control risk is higher than normal

F   Control risk is lower than normal   LO 2b

26   Which TWO of the following are reasons why organisations need to have effective systems of control?

To assist the organisation in

A   Minimising business risks

B   Maximising its profitability

C   Managing its assets and liabilities

D   Cutting down the time needed for the audit

E   Complying with laws and regulations   LO 2a

27   An effective system of internal control requires segregation of basic functions. Which THREE of the following functions should ideally be segregated?

A   Authorisation of transactions

B   Preparation of financial statements

C   Custody or handling of assets

D   Budgetary control

E   Recording of transactions   LO 2b

28   An audit committee is a committee with responsibility for audit related matters comprised of which of the following?

A   Executive directors only

B   Non-executive directors only

C   Non-executive directors and internal auditors

D   Non-executive directors and external auditors   LO 2d

29   ISA 315 states that an internal control system in an organisation consists of five components: the control environment, the entity's risk assessment process, the information system, control activities and monitoring of controls.

For each of the following examples select the component which it illustrates.

The entity's organisational structure

A   Control environment

B   Control activity

C   Monitoring of controls

Review by management of monthly bank reconciliations

D   Control environment

E   Control activity

F   Monitoring of controls   LO 2d

30 The following are examples of internal controls which operate at Fairweather plc. For each example select the type of control activity which it illustrates.

The financial accountant signs the bank reconciliation, which has been prepared by a member of his staff

A   Authorisation

B   Performance review

The finance director compares monthly expenditure on consumables to budgeted expenditure

C   Authorisation

D   Performance review   LO 2e

31 Most entities make use of IT systems for financial reporting and operational purposes. Controls operating in an IT environment can be split into general controls and application controls. Which of the following is an application control?

A   Use of passwords

B   Testing of new systems

C   Authorisation of data for input

D   Disaster recovery plan   LO 2e

32 Which TWO of the following will reduce password effectiveness as a means of restricting access to a computer system?

A   Frequent changes of passwords

B   User selection of passwords

C   Automatic disconnection after failed attempts to access system

D   Disciplinary offence if passwords revealed

E   Displaying the password on screen   LO 2f

Chapter 6: Revenue system

1 Which THREE of the following are risks associated with the sales system?

   A   Orders may be taken from customers who are not able to pay

   B   Goods may be despatched but not invoiced

   C   The full credit period offered might not be taken

   D   Money might be received at the premises but not banked   LO 2c

2 Which TWO of the following controls best mitigate the risk that customers might not be able to pay?

   A   Authorisation of credit terms to customers

   B   Obtaining customers' signatures on delivery documentation

   C   Regular preparation of trade receivables statements

   D   Checking the ageing of the current receivables ledger balance prior to accepting orders   LO 2f

3 Which THREE of the following controls best **prevent** misappropriation of customers' remittances?

   A   Segregation of duties between cash handling and recording

   B   Post opening by two people

   C   Investigation of differences between till records and cash collected

   D   Regular banking   LO 2f

4 The following describes the processes which make up the sales system in operation at Sheraton and Co.

   For each process, select whether it represents a strength or a deficiency of the system.

   Orders are placed by telephone. When a call is received, the person receiving the order checks that the customer's credit status supports the order and that the customer's current balance is below the maximum level and then immediately inputs the order into the system.

   A   Strength

   B   Deficiency

   The order automatically generates a message to the distribution centre which despatches the goods and to the accounts department, which immediately raises an invoice and sends it to the customer.

   C   Strength

   D   Deficiency

   Customer queries are dealt with by reception staff.

   E   Strength

   F   Deficiency   LO 2g/h

5   Select whether each of the following statements is true or false.

In the sales system, the following duties should be segregated:

Recording sales and access to remittances from customers

A   True

B   False

Credit control and invoicing

C   True

D   False   LO 2b

6   The internal auditor at Windsor Ltd has identified the following deficiencies within that organisation's sales system.

For each deficiency select the most likely consequence which might arise as a result of that deficiency.

Invoices are matched to orders but not warehouse records

A   Customers may not pay promptly

B   Invoices may be raised in error

C   Orders may be accepted from customers who are unable to pay

Receivables statements are not sent to customers

D   Customers may not pay promptly

E   Invoices may be raised in error

F   Orders may be accepted from customers who are unable to pay   LO 2f/h

7   The external auditor at Reading Ltd has identified the following deficiencies within that organisation's sales system.

For each deficiency select the most likely consequence which might arise as a result of that deficiency.

Overdue accounts are not followed up

A   Invoiced sales might not be properly recorded

B   Credit notes might not be properly recorded

C   Debts might be included on the receivables ledger that are not collectable

Invoices are not in numerical sequence

D   Invoiced sales might not be properly recorded

E   Credit notes might not be properly recorded

F   Debts might be included on the receivables ledger that are not collectable   LO 2f/h

8   Which TWO of the following are risks associated with the sales system?

    A   Orders may be taken from customers who are not able to pay

    B   Invoices may be cancelled by valid credit notes

    C   Goods may be received but not invoiced

    D   Sales might be recorded in the wrong customer accounts   LO 2c

9   Bourne Ltd operates a number of control procedures in its sales system.

    Assuming that all controls are operating effectively, which of the following control procedures is MOST likely to ensure that customers are invoiced for goods received?

    A   Use of pre-printed sequentially numbered sales order documentation

    B   Matching of sales orders with despatch notes

    C   Matching of despatch notes with sales invoices

    D   Requiring customers to sign for goods received   LO 2f

10 The following describes aspects of the sales system in operation at Barrow plc.

    For each process select whether it represents a strength or a deficiency of the system.

    Sales invoices are matched to despatch notes and sales orders. The calculations on the invoices are checked by the accounts clerk.

    A   Strength

    B   Deficiency

    The receivables ledger clerk posts the sales invoices and cash received to the receivables ledger. The receivables ledger clerk also reconciles the receivables ledger to the control account on a monthly basis.

    C   Strength

    D   Deficiency

    The condition of goods returned is checked and a goods returned note is produced. A copy of this is sent to the accounts department and a credit note is raised by the chief accountant.

    E   Strength

    F   Deficiency   LO 2g/h

11 The following deficiencies have been identified in two separate sales systems.

For each deficiency, select the most likely consequence which might arise as a result of that deficiency.

Despatch documentation is not sequentially pre-numbered

A   Sales may be made to customers who cannot pay

B   Invoices may not be raised for all goods despatched

C   Customers may not pay promptly

Customers are not required to evidence receipt of goods

D   Sales may be made to customers who cannot pay

E   Invoices may not be raised for all goods despatched

F   Customers may not pay promptly   LO 2f/h

---

12 Which TWO of the following are objectives of the sales ordering part of the sales system?

A   Sales are only made to credit worthy customers

B   Goods are correctly invoiced

C   Cut-off is correct

D   Orders can be fulfilled   LO 2c

---

13 The following describes the processes which make up the sales system in operation at Raffles and Co.

For each process select whether it represents a strength or a deficiency of the system.

Orders are placed by telephone. On receipt of a call, following credit checks, the order is immediately entered onto the system.

A   Strength

B   Deficiency

The order generates a despatch note which is forwarded to the warehouse and an invoice which is forwarded to accounts receivable. Goods in inventory are despatched immediately and the despatch note is amended manually for unavailable goods.

C   Strength

D   Deficiency

A copy of any despatch notes with incomplete orders is filed in an 'unfulfilled orders' file which is reviewed daily and the backlog filled as soon as inventory is available.

E   Strength

F   Deficiency   LO 2g/h

1   For each of the following examples, select the type of internal control activity which it represents.

Monthly management accounts are compared to budget and differences investigated

A   Authorisation

B   Performance review

C   Information processing

Numerical sequence checks are undertaken on goods received records

D   Authorisation

E   Performance review

F   Information processing   LO 2e

2   The auditor of Twickenham Ltd has identified the following deficiencies within that organisation's accounting system.

For each deficiency select the most likely consequence which might arise as a result of that deficiency.

Goods inwards are not checked

A   Accepting inferior quality goods

B   False invoices could be paid

C   Services received are not accurately recorded.

Invoices are not checked to original orders

D   Accepting inferior quality goods

E   False invoices could be paid

F   Services received are not accurately recorded   LO 2f/h

3   The following describes the processes which make up the purchases system at Hawthorns and Co.

For each process select whether it represents a strength or a deficiency of the system.

Orders are placed by department heads, usually by telephone, when they determine a service is required.

A   Strength

B   Deficiency

Invoices for services are checked against the service provider's proof of delivery of service, which is requested from every service provider.

C   Strength

D   Deficiency

Payments are made by direct transfer. The direct transfer list is authorised by the financial controller, who verifies the payments to supporting documents, such as the invoice or service agreement.

E   Strength

F   Deficiency   LO 2g/h

4   Redesign Ltd is a large property management company which makes use of the services of many different contractors for building, design and decorating services.

Which TWO of the following internal controls are most likely to **prevent** services being used for the private purposes of employees

A   Purchase orders are processed by the buying department following authorisation by the production director

B   Purchase requisitions must be signed by two team members for any given project

C   Purchase orders should only be placed with authorised contractors

D   Purchase invoices are matched to authorised purchase orders   LO 2f

5   The organisational structure at Molyneux Ltd is as follows. The production department is headed by Jack Frost, whose deputy is Tiny Tim. Jack Frost reports to the managing director, Nicholas Clause. There are several other departments (sales and marketing, accounting, purchasing, HR and internal audit).

Which of the following statements reflects the ideal situation with regard to purchase ordering?

A   Jack Frost and Tiny Tim should make purchase orders as production needs dictate

B   Jack Frost should make purchase orders, although Tiny Tim could make requisitions as production needs dictate

C   Jack Frost and Tiny Tim should requisition materials as production needs dictate, but orders should be placed by the purchasing department

D   Jack Frost and Tiny Tim should requisition materials as production needs dictate but orders should be placed by the purchasing department, having been authorised by Nicholas Clause
                                                                                           LO 2g

6   Grey Ltd has recently discovered that it has been paying invoices in respect of goods which had been returned as faulty prior to acceptance. It is company policy to record goods only if they have been accepted.

Which of the following controls would have prevented this from occurring?

A   Matching of purchase invoices with goods received notes

B   Matching of purchase invoices with orders

C   Comparison of supplier statements with payables ledger accounts

D   Date stamping purchase invoices on receipt   LO 2f

7   The following are examples of deficiencies in the purchases system of Burns Ltd.

For each example, select the type of internal control activity which would improve the system.

Errors have been made in the calculation of discounts receivable

A   Authorisation

B   Physical controls

C   Information processing

There has been increasing levels of theft from the main distribution centre

D   Authorisation

E   Physical controls

F   Information processing   LO 2f

8   Which TWO of the following deficiencies identified in the purchases system of Harrow Ltd could result in a misstatement of liabilities?

A   The buying department does not always use authorised suppliers

B   Harrow Ltd does not always take advantage of prompt payment discounts

C   Purchase invoices are not matched with goods received notes

D   The payables ledger is not reconciled to the payables ledger control account   LO 2f/h

9   The auditor of Rainer Ltd has identified the following deficiencies within that organisation's accounting system.

For each deficiency select the MOST LIKELY consequence which might arise as a result of that deficiency.

Purchase of goods from unauthorised suppliers

A   Payment to fictitious suppliers

B   Purchase of inferior goods

C   Prompt payment discounts not obtained

Purchase ledger clerks permitted to amend standing data on the payables master file

D   Payment to fictitious suppliers

E   Purchase of inferior goods

F   Prompt payment discounts not obtained   LO 2f/h

1   Hire Company Ltd uses a lot of temporary employees.

Which of the following controls would BEST ENSURE that employees are only paid for work they have performed?

A   Temporary staff records should be maintained for each member of temporary staff

B   Temporary staff should complete work schedules, authorised by their supervisor

C   Temporary staff pay should be authorised by the human resources manager

D   Temporary staff should be paid by direct transfers to their bank accounts   LO 2f

2   Tulips Ltd has a number of staff on maternity leave claiming statutory maternity pay.

Which THREE of the following controls would BEST ENSURE that the correct payments are made to employees?

A   The payroll should be checked back to individual employee personnel records

B   Payroll totals should be compared to adjusted budgets on a monthly basis

C   Total tax deductions should be reconciled with tax returns

D   BACS transfer lists should be authorised by the head of personnel   LO 2f

3   For each of the following statements, select whether they are true or false in respect of internal controls over payroll.

Requiring employees to clock in and out of work helps to ensure that they are paid at the correct rate

A   True

B   False

Reviewing wages paid against wages budgeted helps to ensure that employees are being paid the correct amounts

C   True

D   False

Changes in pay rates should be authorised by senior management

E   True

F   False   LO 2f

4   Stamford plc employs a number of trainee staff, at six monthly intervals. All trainees must complete a probationary period of six months before progressing to the next level of traineeship. The accountant providing assurance on the efficiency of the operation of controls has identified the following deficiencies within Stamford Ltd's payroll system.

For each deficiency select the MOST LIKELY consequence which might arise as a result of that deficiency.

Employees are not given a personnel file until they have completed their six month probationary period

A   Employees may be paid the wrong amounts

B   The computerised payroll may contain miscalculations

Many employees work overtime but there is no system for authorising the levels of overtime claimed

C   Employees may be paid the wrong amounts

D   The computerised payroll may contain miscalculations   LO 2f/h

---

5   The following describes the processes in the payroll system at Wembley Ltd.

For each process, select whether it represents a strength or a deficiency of the system.

Employees are given individual security codes to punch into the main door key pad. This key pad also monitors the hours worked by employees

A   Strength

B   Deficiency

The payroll is prepared by a payroll clerk from hours worked information on a standard payroll IT package. The payroll is checked to individual records automatically by the system. The payroll is approved by the financial controller

C   Strength

D   Deficiency

Wages are paid by bank transfer, which is authorised by the financial controller

E   Strength

F   Deficiency   LO 2g/h

---

6   Workworld Ltd maintains a computerised payroll system. All employees are paid by BACS directly into their bank account.

Which TWO of the following controls will be most effective in ensuring that payment is made to the correct employee?

A   Authorisation of overtime worked

B   A sample of calculations performed by the payroll package are manually reperformed each month

C   The BACS list is reviewed by the chief accountant together with supporting payroll documentation

D   The print out from the bank is agreed to the BACS list and any discrepancies investigated

                                                                                          LO 2f

---

7 Which TWO of the following features in the payroll system of Tyne plc could result in the employee costs figure in the financial statements being misstated?

A   Rates of pay are negotiated at a local level, there is no central control

B   The payroll clerk can amend standing data on the payroll system without authorisation of a senior member of staff

C   Personnel records are not kept up to date

D   The payroll department receives confirmation of new employees in writing   LO 2h

8 For each of the following statements, select whether they are true or false in respect of internal controls over payroll.

The payroll should be checked back to individual employee personnel records on a regular basis

A   True

B   False

Leavers and joiners should be authorised by a senior member of staff

C   True

D   False

Reperformance of calculations is unnecessary where the payroll system is computerised

E   True

F   False   LO 2f

9 Spoon Ltd is a company that is expanding rapidly and is regularly taking on new employees. The payroll is processed in-house in the accounts department using a PC. The financial controller is concerned that fictitious employees could be included on the payroll by an unscrupulous employee from the accounts department.

Which of the following internal controls is MOST likely to **prevent** this from happening?

A   Payroll standing data periodically printed out and checked on a line-by-line basis to independently held employee details

B   Use of hierarchical passwords over standing data files

C   Pre-authorisation of all amendments to payroll standing data by an independent official

D   Supervision of the wages payout by an independent official   LO 2f

10 Which TWO of the following control procedures will reduce the risk of unauthorised disclosure of payroll data?

A   Exception reporting of high amounts of net pay

B   Access controls

C   Back-up procedures

D   Encryption of data

E   Independent review of payroll   LO 2f

1   The scope and objectives of the internal audit function vary widely and depend on the size and structure of the entity and the requirements of its management.

Which TWO of the following functions could internal audit perform and still operate effectively?

A   Examination of financial and operating information

B   Review of the company's compliance with laws and regulations

C   Authorisation of unusual transactions

D   Development of internal control systems   LO 2d

2   Which TWO of the following roles could internal audit carry out in respect of risk management and still operate effectively?

A   Monitoring the company's overall risk strategy

B   Designing an internal control system in a production department

C   Testing internal controls in the purchasing department

D   Implementing internal controls in the sales department   LO 2d

3   Which THREE of the following roles could the internal audit function carry out to assist the board in its management of the company and still operate effectively?

A   Carrying out the statutory audit

B   Giving expert advice on technical accounting matters

C   Liaising with the external auditors

D   Auditing board reports not audited by the external auditors   LO 2d

4   Internal audit assists in achieving corporate objectives.

For each of the following statements select whether or not they are true or false.

Having an internal audit function is a requirement of the UK Corporate Governance Code

A   True

B   False

Internal audit can be seen as an internal control in a company

C   True

D   False

Internal auditors should not get involved in operational matters

E   True

F   False   LO 2d

5   For each of the following statements concerning internal audit, select whether they are true or false.

Internal audit can never be independent of those on whom they are reporting, because they are employees of the company

A   True

B   False

All listed companies in the UK are required by the UK Corporate Governance Code to have an internal audit function

C   True

D   False

Internal audit focuses on the efficiency and effectiveness of a company's operations by testing its internal controls. They do not carry out substantive testing

E   True

F   False   LO 2d

6   Hiltson Hotels is a global group of hotels. The parent company, Hiltson Holdings plc employs an internal audit function which carries out audits and investigations on the individual hotels in the group.

Which TWO of the following could the internal audit function carry out and still operate effectively?

A   Secondment to the accounts department of the Singapore Hiltson to cover the maternity leave of the financial controller

B   Special investigation into the profits of the New York Hiltson where the group directors suspect a fraud may have been carried out

C   Tests of the controls at the Edinburgh Hiltson as part of a routine internal audit cycle

D   Identification of risks at the proposed Nairobi Hiltson, which is due to open in nine months' time

LO 2d

7   Internal and external auditors provide different services to companies.

For each of the following examples select whether it is a service which would be provided by internal auditors only, by external auditors only or by either.

Statutory audit

A   Internal auditors

B   External auditors

C   Either

Monitoring of internal controls

D   Internal auditors

E   External auditors

F   Either   LO 2d

8   Many of the procedures undertaken by the internal auditor are very similar to those performed by the external auditor.

Which of the following procedures will NOT be performed by the internal auditor if he is to still operate effectively?

A   Monitoring of internal controls

B   Making recommendations regarding improvements to controls

C   Examining and testing financial information

D   Expressing an opinion on the truth and fairness of the financial statements   LO 2d

9   Which of the following best describes the term 'operational audit'?

A   Any audit performed by the internal auditor

B   An audit of the operational processes of the organisation

C   An audit performed by the operations director

D   A statutory audit   LO 2d

10   To which TWO of the following parties would the internal auditor report?

A   Board of directors

B   Shareholders

C   Audit committee

D   External auditors   LO 2d

11   Which THREE of the following activities would typically be performed by BOTH the internal and external auditor?

A   Review of compliance with laws and regulations

B   Assessment of the effectiveness of internal controls

C   Review of the efficiency of operations

D   Carrying out tests of details on transactions and balances   LO 2d

12   The scope and objectives of the internal audit function vary widely and depend on the size and structure of the entity and the requirements of its management.

Which THREE of the following functions could internal audit perform and still operate effectively?

A   Examination of financial and operational information for management

B   Authorisation of transactions in excess of limits set by management

C   Review of accounting systems and related controls

D   Advising management on cost effective controls for systems and activities

E   Routinely preparing bank reconciliations   LO 2d

Assurance: Question Bank

Chapter 10: Documentation

1   Which of the following is NOT a reason that assurance providers record their work?

    A   To confirm the terms of the engagement

    B   To assist the assurance team to plan and perform the engagement

    C   To retain a record of matters of continuing significance to the engagement

    D   To enable an experienced assurance provider to carry out quality control reviews   LO 3a

2   Which THREE of the following should working papers show?

    A   The name of the client

    B   The date the work was planned

    C   The date the work was carried out

    D   The date the work was reviewed

    E   The initials of the person supervising the work   LO 1f

3   Which TWO of the following are likely to be kept on a permanent audit file?

    A   Engagement letter

    B   Planning memorandum

    C   Review notes

    D   Previous year's signed financial statements

    E   Current year's draft financial statements   LO 1f

4   Which TWO of the following statements are correct?

    A   Working papers belong to the assurance provider

    B   Working papers should be kept for the current and previous year only

    C   Working papers should not be made available to third parties without client permission

    D   Working papers should be made available to third parties at the request of the client   LO 1f

5   The assurance provider will prepare documentation in relation to the fieldwork carried out on an assurance engagement.

For each of the following select whether or not they are valid reasons for preparing such documentation.

To retain a record of matters of continuing significance to future engagements

A   Valid

B   Not valid

To fulfil legal requirements covering assurance providers

C   Valid

D   Not valid

To enable quality control reviews to be carried out

E   Valid

F   Not valid   LO 3a

6   Many auditors use two types of audit file: a current audit file and a permanent audit file.

For each of the following documents select the file or files which that document is most likely to be filed in.

Engagement letter

A   Current audit file

B   Permanent audit file

C   Both

Audit plan

D   Current audit file

E   Permanent audit file

F   Both

Manager review notes

G   Current audit file

H   Permanent audit file

I   Both   LO 1f

7   Which THREE of the following documents would be held on a current audit file?

A   Details of the history of the client's business

B   Communications with experts

C   Audit file review notes

D   Copies of management accounts

E   Lease agreements   LO 1f

8   For each of the following statements select whether they are true or false.

Working papers should be stored in locked premises

A   True

B   False

An auditor can destroy the audit plan relating to Jacobs Ltd for the year ended 30 June 20X3 in 20Y0

C   True

D   False

Working papers belong to the client and may be stored at their premises

E   True

F   False   LO 1f

9   For each of the following select whether or not they are valid reasons for preparing audit working papers.

To assist the audit team to plan and perform the audit

A   Valid

B   Not valid

To enable the auditor to charge a higher fee

C   Valid

D   Not valid

To prove adherence to ISAs

E   Valid

F   Not valid   LO 3a

10 The assurance provider will prepare documentation in relation to the fieldwork carried out on an assurance engagement.

For each of the following select whether or not they are valid reasons for preparing such documentation.

To assist in establishing the overall audit strategy for this year's engagement

A   Valid

B   Not valid

To assist in this year's review process

C   Valid

D   Not valid

To provide a record of evidence gathered to support the conclusions reached

E   Valid

F   Not valid   LO 3a

11 Many auditors use two types of audit file: a permanent audit file and a current audit file.

For each of the following types of information select the appropriate file in which it will be contained.

Audit strategy document

A   Permanent audit file

B   Current audit file

Written representation from management

C   Permanent audit file

D   Current audit file

Accounting systems notes

E   Permanent audit file

F   Current audit file   LO 1f

12 Which THREE of the following are advantages of automated working papers?

A   They may result in substantial time-savings

B   The risk of errors is reduced

C   The auditor does not need to apply judgement in assessing the results

D   They will be easier to review   LO 1f

13 Which of the following statements is correct in respect of the minimum period, as required by the ICAEW, for which audit working papers must be retained by the auditor?

A   Five years from the date of completion of the audit work

B   Six years from the date of the auditor's report

C   Six years from the end of the accounting period to which they relate

D   Five years from the date of approval of the financial statements by the shareholders   LO 1f

14 Which of the following statements is correct in respect of the safe custody of audit documentation?

A   Whilst audit documentation is held on the client's premises it is the responsibility of the client to ensure its safe custody

B   The auditor need only ensure the safe custody of audit documentation for the duration of the audit

C   The auditor must ensure the safe custody of audit documentation for at least six years from the end of the accounting period to which it relates

D   All audit documentation must be destroyed within five years of the end of the accounting period to which it relates   LO 1f

Chapter 11: Evidence and sampling

1   Which TWO of the following statements are correct?

   A   Inspection of assets confirms rights and obligations

   B   Inspection of a purchase invoice confirms the cost of inventory

   C   Observation gives strong ongoing evidence of the matter being observed

   D   Inquiry of third parties gives better evidence than inquiries of entity insiders   LO 3d

2   In which THREE of the following situations could audit software appropriately be used?

   A   To check calculations on a selection of invoices

   B   To extract a sample of invoices over a certain value

   C   To extract all invoices to specific customers

   D   To test controls over invoice processing   LO 3d

3   According to ISAs 315 and 520 which TWO of the following statements are correct?

   A   Analytical procedures must be used as risk assessment procedures

   B   Analytical procedures must be used as substantive procedures

   C   Analytical procedures must be used during the overall review stage of an audit

   D   Analytical procedures must be carried out by senior level assurance staff   LO 3d

4   Which THREE of the following statements are correct?

   When using analytical procedures, assurance providers should

   A   Consider whether the information they might require will be available

   B   Consider the knowledge gained during previous assurance engagements

   C   Consider the source of the information and whether it is reliable

   D   Not use information that has been internally generated at the entity   LO 3e

5   Which of the following procedures would be the most appropriate for verifying the interest accrued on borrowings?

   A   Confirming the interest rate with the lender

   B   Vouching the payment of interest on the borrowings

   C   Testing internal controls over cash payments

   D   Recalculating the interest accrued on the basis of outstanding amount, interest rate and period to which it relates   LO 3d

6   Which TWO of the following statements are correct?

   A   When testing for overstatement, the assurance provider will test items from the accounting records to the supporting documents

   B   When testing for understatement, the assurance provider will test items from the accounting records to the supporting documents

   C   When testing for overstatement, the assurance provider will select items from outside the accounting records and trace to the records

   D   When testing for understatement, the assurance provider will select items from outside the accounting records and trace to the records   LO 3f

7   Which TWO of the following constitute sampling?

   A   Testing 100% of the items in a population

   B   Testing less than 100% of the items in a population

   C   Testing all items with a certain characteristic

   D   Testing items selected randomly from the population   LO 3b

8   Which TWO of the following are factors that an assurance provider should take into account when determining the sample size for a test of details?

   A   The time available to complete the test

   B   The skill of the team member assigned to carry out the test

   C   A decrease in the assurance provider's assessment of the risk of material misstatement

   D   An increase in the level of expected misstatement   LO 3g

9   Which THREE of the following methods would be most appropriate to use to select a sample of accounts receivable when the assurance provider is using statistical sampling?

   A   Random selection

   B   Systematic selection

   C   Haphazard selection

   D   Sequence selection

   E   Monetary unit selection   LO 3f

10 Which TWO of the following misstatements discovered in a sample would not generally be extrapolated against the total population?

   A   A misposting between customer accounts

   B   A misstatement in invoice value

   C   An invoice omitted in error

   D   An invoice disputed by a customer

   E   A timing difference between customer records and client records   LO 3g

11 Assurance providers obtain evidence using procedures set out in ISA 500.

For each of the following tests select the type of procedure which is being used.

The assurance provider writes to a sample of customers asking them to inform him of the balance they owe the company at the year end

A Inspection

B Observation

C Confirmation

The assurance provider looks at a share certificate to confirm that the company has an investment in Company A

D Inspection

E Observation

F Confirmation

The assurance provider attends the inventory count and ensures that it is being carried out in accordance with the issued instructions

G Inspection

H Observation

I Confirmation   LO 3f

12 For each of the following statements concerning computer assisted audit techniques select whether they are true or false.

Computer assisted audit techniques can be used to perform the assurance procedure of 'reperformance'

A True

B False

Test data can be used to ensure that controls in the client's system are operating as the assurance provider expects them to

C True

D False

Audit software makes use of the client's specialised software to run audit procedures

E True

F False   LO 3b

13 In respect of an assurance engagement which of the following is the LEAST persuasive method of gathering evidence?

A Inspection of a supplier's invoice

B Reperformance of a supplier statement reconciliation obtained from the client

C Reperformance of a depreciation calculation undertaken by the reporting accountant

D Inspection of a sales invoice produced by the client   LO 3e

14   When determining a sample size for tests of details there are a number of factors which an auditor should take into account.

For each of the following factors, select whether it would cause the sample size to increase or to decrease.

The auditor's required confidence level increases

A   Increase

B   Decrease

The assessed risk of a material misstatement in respect of a balance has been reappraised and has increased

C   Increase

D   Decrease

The population has been stratified

E   Increase

F   Decrease   LO 3g

15   When determining a sample size for tests of controls, there are a number of factors which an auditor should take into account.

For each of the following factors select whether it would cause the sample size to increase, decrease, or to have negligible effect.

An increase in tolerable misstatement

A   Increase

B   Decrease

C   Negligible effect

An increase in the number of invoices in the population

D   Increase

E   Decrease

F   Negligible effect

A decrease in the auditor's required confidence level

G   Increase

H   Decrease

I   Negligible effect   LO 3g

16   Which TWO of the following statements are correct regarding factors which influence sample sizes for tests of controls?

A   An increase in the number of sampling units within the population will increase the sample size

B   A decrease in the expected misstatement will decrease the sample size

C   A decrease in the tolerable misstatement will decrease the sample size

D   An increase in the extent to which the risk of material misstatement is reduced by the operating effectiveness of controls will increase the sample size   LO 3g

17 For each of the following statements select whether they are true or false in respect of procedures to obtain evidence.

Physical examination of property, plant and equipment confirms ownership

A   True

B   False

Recalculation is a strong form of evidence as it is created by the assurance provider

C   True

D   False

Inquiry is always an unreliable means of obtaining evidence

E   True

F   False   LO 3d

18 For each of the following pieces of evidence select whether it is more reliable or less reliable than the piece of evidence it is paired with.

A sales invoice is more reliable/less reliable than a purchase invoice

A   More reliable

B   Less reliable

An original copy of a lease agreement is more reliable/less reliable than a photocopy

C   More reliable

D   Less reliable

A bank statement is more reliable/less reliable than a cash book

E   More reliable

F   Less reliable   LO 3e

19 All methods of obtaining evidence have deficiencies. Examples of such deficiencies are listed below.

For each deficiency select the method of obtaining evidence which is most likely to result in that deficiency.

Limited to the point in time it takes place

A   Analytical review

B   Observation of a procedure

Limited by underlying accounting system

C   Analytical review

D   Observation of a procedure

A balance which is overstated may be agreed because it favours the respondent

E   Direct confirmation of a receivables balance

F   Direct confirmation of a payables balance   LO 3c

20 In accordance with ISAs 315 and 520 select whether analytical procedures are compulsory or optional in each of the following circumstances.

At the risk assessment stage of the audit

A   Compulsory

B   Optional

As a substantive procedure

C   Compulsory

D   Optional

At the overall review stage of the audit

E   Compulsory

F   Optional   LO 3d

21 Which TWO of the following circumstances would REDUCE the reliability of the results of analytical procedures?

A   Detailed information is available analysed by department

B   Budgeted figures in the past have proved to be highly optimistic

C   Reliable industry data is available

D   Significant deficiencies in the internal control system have been identified in the past   LO 3e

22 Which TWO of the following procedures describe tests for understatement?

A   Selecting a sample of despatch notes and tracing these to a matching sales invoice and entry in the sales account

B   Selecting a sample of sales invoices and tracing these to a matching despatch note

C   Selecting a sample of items of plant physically verified by the assurance provider and tracing these to an entry in the asset register

D   Selecting a sample of items of plant from the asset register and physically verifying their existence

                                                                                LO 3f

23 The auditor of Frost Ltd has carried out a test on a sample of receivables and has discovered a higher than expected number of misstatements.

Which THREE of the following steps would be an appropriate response to this?

A   Investigate the nature and cause of the misstatements

B   Consider the effect of the misstatements on other parts of the audit

C   Estimate the probable overall misstatement by extrapolating the results

D   Increase the tolerable misstatement   LO 3g

24   When determining a sample size for tests of details there are a number of factors which an auditor should take into account.

For each of the following factors select whether it would cause the sample size to increase or to decrease.

An increase in the auditor's assessment of the risk of material misstatement

A   Increase

B   Decrease

An increase in the use of analytical procedures to test the same assertion

C   Increase

D   Decrease

An increase in the level of misstatements that the auditor expects to find when testing the assertion

E   Increase

F   Decrease   LO 3g

25   For each of the procedures below, select whether the auditor will be testing primarily for overstatement or primarily for understatement.

Communicating with the client's legal advisers for details about outstanding legal claims

A   Primarily for overstatement of provisions

B   Primarily for understatement of provisions

Reviewing the aged inventory analysis to identify old/obsolete inventory

C   Primarily for overstatement of inventory

D   Primarily for understatement of inventory

The auditor calculating for himself the warranty provision and comparing their figure to the balance stated in the balance sheet

E   Primarily for overstatement of warranty provision

F   Primarily for understatement of warranty provision   LO 3f

26   For each of the following statements select whether they are true or false in respect of test data.

Test data is a type of substantive procedure

A   True

B   False

Test data can include real data and dummy data

C   True

D   False

Test data can be used to assist in the calculation of ratios

E   True

F   False   LO 3b

27 Which of the following is the definition of an anomaly?

A   A misstatement or deviation that is demonstrably not representative of misstatements or deviations in a population

B   The misstatement that the auditor expects to be present in the population

C   Control deviations, when performing tests of control, or misstatements, when performing substantive procedures

D   The maximum misstatement in the population that the auditor would be willing to accept LO 3g

28 For each of the following descriptions select whether they describe monetary unit sampling, block selection or systematic selection.

Peter is auditing trade accounts receivable. Materiality is £25,000. The sample is selected on the basis of choosing the balances containing each $25,000^{th}$ £1 on a cumulative basis.

A   Monetary unit sampling

B   Block selection

C   Systematic selection

Paul is checking whether purchase invoices have been authorised for payment. He has selected all the November purchase invoices as his sample and has reviewed them for an authorisation signature.

D   Monetary unit sampling

E   Block selection

F   Systematic selection   LO 3b

29 In order to gather sufficient, appropriate evidence, the auditor may make use of external confirmation requests.

For each of the following statements with regards to external confirmation requests select whether it is true or false.

A positive confirmation request always asks the respondents to reply to the auditor indicating whether or not they agree with the information provided

A   True

B   False

A sample of confirmation requests drawn from the client's list of balances is more appropriate for receivables balances than for payables balances

C   True

D   False

A positive confirmation request ordinarily provides more reliable audit evidence than a negative confirmation request

E   True

F   False   LO 3c

1   According to ISA 580 which THREE of the following is an auditor required to confirm in writing with management?

A   Management's belief that it has fulfilled its responsibility for the preparation of financial statements

B   All transactions have been reflected in the financial statements

C   The fact that management has provided the auditor with all relevant information

D   Management's agreement of the level of materiality used during the audit   LO 3h

2   According to ISA 580 which TWO of the following must auditors obtain written representations about?

A   Material matters where other evidence cannot reasonably be expected to exist

B   Material matters where other evidence is missing due to an emergency such as a fire

C   Management's belief that it has fulfilled its responsibility for the preparation of the financial statements

D   That the financial statements record and reflect all transactions   LO 3h

3   For each of the following statements concerning written representations select whether they are true or false.

The auditor should evaluate whether the representations appear reliable and are consistent with other evidence obtained before they are relied on as audit evidence

A   True

B   False

Written representations are appropriate evidence when evidence the auditors expected to be available is unavailable

C   True

D   False

If written representations given do not agree with other evidence, auditors should not trust any other representations made by management during the course of the audit

E   True

F   False   LO 3h

4   Auditors seek written representations from management to support oral representations that have been made during the course of the audit.

For each of the following in relation to a statutory audit select whether a written representation is required or not required.

The directors have fulfilled their responsibility for the preparation of the financial statements

A   Required

B   Not required

The accounting policies selected and applied by management are appropriate

C   Required

D   Not required

A material item, subject to management judgement, for which no other evidence could reasonably be expected to exist

E   Required

F   Not required   LO 3h

5   Written representations may be sought as audit evidence.

Which TWO of the following are valid circumstances in which written representations may be required?

A   To support other evidence about the suitability of accounting policies

B   Where information which would normally be expected to be available is unavailable

C   To support inspection of a board minute introducing the directors' intention to sell a material investment

D   When the alternative audit procedure would be too time consuming   LO 3h

6   On which TWO of the following matters should an auditor seek written representations?

A   Whether there are plans to abandon product lines that will result in obsolete inventory

B   Whether plant and equipment held on the client's premises exists

C   The existence (or not) of reconciling items between the cash balance and the bank statement balance

D   Whether there are any undisclosed subsequent events   LO 3h

7   For each of the following statements concerning written representation letters select whether they are true or false.

A written representation letter is only required for new clients

A   True

B   False

The written representation letter must be dated before the audit report

C   True

D   False

The written representation letter must include a list of all uncorrected misstatements

E   True

F   False   LO 3h

8   For each of the following statements concerning written representation letters select whether they are true or false.

Written confirmations are required from all client staff who have made oral representations

A   True

B   False

The matters to be referred to in the written representation letter shall be discussed by the auditor with senior management

C   True

D   False

Written representations can be used as a substitute for evidence which would be available to the auditor by other means

E   True

F   False   LO 3h

9   Which TWO of the following are purposes of a written representation letter?

A   Acknowledgement that management has fulfilled its responsibility for the preparation of the financial statements

B   Provision of evidence in respect of material items where other evidence is available

C   Acknowledgement by management of its belief that the aggregate of uncorrected misstatements are immaterial to the financial statements

D   Confirmation by management of the scope of the work to be carried out by the assurance firm

E   To provide details of proposed modifications to the auditor's report   LO 3h

1   Which THREE of the following provide evidence to support the rights and obligations assertion in relation to non-current assets?

   A   Title deeds

   B   Purchase invoices

   C   Vehicle registration documents

   D   Sales invoices   LO 3d

2   Which of the following assertions is the assurance provider LEAST concerned with when testing a non-current asset balance?

   A   Existence

   B   Rights and obligations

   C   Completeness

   D   Cut-off   LO 3d

3   Which THREE of the following are the more significant risks in relation to an inventory balance in the financial statements?

   A   Inventory exists but has not been included in the financial statements

   B   Inventory has been valued at cost when net realisable value is lower

   C   Inventory has been valued when it is obsolete and has no value

   D   Inventory has not been disclosed properly in the financial statements   LO 3d

4   Which TWO of the following constitute the BEST quality evidence concerning the net realisable value of inventory?

   A   Company's controls over inventory counting

   B   Post year-end sales invoices

   C   Post year-end sales orders

   D   Post year-end sales price list   LO 3e

5   Which of the following is the reason why the positive method of confirming receivables balances with customers is generally preferred?

    A   It is carried out in the auditor's name

    B   It requires the customer to reply giving or confirming or disagreeing with the balance

    C   It only requires the customer to reply if he disagrees with the balance

    D   It requires replies to be sent to the client   LO 3e

6   Which TWO of the following procedures are MOST appropriate to confirm the valuation of trade receivables?

    A   Review of the receivables ledger

    B   Direct confirmations with customers

    C   Review of cash paid after date

    D   Review of sales invoices   LO 3d

7   Which of the following procedures which could be undertaken to confirm the valuation of a client's bank balance is the MOST reliable?

    A   Inspection of the bank reconciliation

    B   Inspection of the bank statement

    C   Inspection of the bank letter

    D   Inspection of the cash book   LO 3e

8   In which TWO of the following situations should an auditor carry out a cash count?

    A   An individual cash float is material

    B   A client has a large number of cash floats, which are immaterial in total

    C   A client has poor controls over cash floats, which are immaterial in total

    D   The auditor suspects that a fraud has been committed in relation to immaterial cash floats   LO 3d

9   Which of the following is the key assertion with which auditors are concerned in relation to payables?

    A   Completeness

    B   Existence

    C   Accuracy

    D   Disclosure   LO 3d

10   Which THREE of the following are reasons why the auditors might seek direct confirmation of balances due from suppliers?

   A   To obtain third party evidence

   B   The auditors suspect that the client is deliberately understating payables

   C   The internal controls relating to purchases are weak

   D   Supplier statements are unavailable   LO 3d

11   Which TWO of the following are reasons why sales are often verified by testing the internal controls in place over sales?

   A   There are usually too many individual transactions to test them individually

   B   Sales constitute a high volume of similar transactions which are suitable for controls testing

   C   Controls over sales in a company are often strong

   D   Because there are so many individual transactions, there is a significant risk that sales are misstated   LO 3b

12   Which THREE of the following relationships/ratios are reasons why analytical procedures can give strong evidence in relation to the accuracy of purchases?

   A   Operating margin

   B   Purchases and payables

   C   Purchases and inventories

   D   Gross margin   LO 3g

13   The results of substantive tests in relation to non-current assets at Hammersmith plc are set out below. The materiality threshold set for these tests was £5,000.

   For each of the following results select the action which should be taken by the audit senior.

   A sample of three assets worth £2,000 in total had been excluded from the non-current asset register and the financial statements

   A   Draw conclusion

   B   Refer to senior colleague

   C   Extend sample

   A building revalued to £100,000 during the year was vouched to an expert valuation carried out by a firm of chartered surveyors

   D   Draw conclusion

   E   Refer to senior colleague

   F   Extend sample   LO 3i

14 The results of substantive tests on trade payables at Fulham Ltd are set out below. The materiality threshold set for these tests was £17,000.

For each of the following results, select the action which should be taken by the audit senior.

Three goods inwards notes dated prior to the year end relating to goods worth £16,000 were traced to purchase invoices which have been included in the subsequent year and not provided for this year.

A   Draw conclusion

B   Refer to senior colleague

C   Extend sample

In a sample of 20 supplier statement reconciliations, statements were unavailable for 10 suppliers. Statements were available for 7 of these 10 suppliers in the previous year.

D   Draw conclusion

E   Refer to senior colleague

F   Extend sample   LO 3i

15 The auditor of Barnett plc carried out an external confirmation of receivables at the year end to confirm the accuracy of total trade receivables in the statement of financial position at that date. Two of the replies to the confirmations disagreed the balance.

For each of these two disagreements, select whether the disagreement would be considered a misstatement or would not be considered a misstatement for the purposes of evaluating the accuracy of total trade receivables in the statement of financial position at the year end.

Watford Ltd disagreed the balance because they had made a payment two days before the year end. The auditor has confirmed that the cheque cleared the bank two days after the year end

A   Misstatement

B   Not misstatement

Radlet Ltd disagreed the balance because their records did not contain invoice number SI 00492. This invoice and associated goods were despatched by Barnett plc on the last day of the year. The auditor has verified that the despatch note and cut-off with inventory are correct

C   Misstatement

D   Not misstatement   LO 3g

16 Hayley, an audit junior, has carried out the following tests to verify the valuation of inventory in the financial statements of Cobham plc.

In each case, select whether the test proves the assertion of valuation or not.

Attending the inventory count and carrying out sample counts on a number of items

A   Proves valuation

B   Does not prove valuation

Comparing cost on a number of inventory items to sales invoices subsequent to the year end

C   Proves valuation

D   Does not prove valuation   LO 3d

17 Lisa has obtained a list of items which make up the cash and cash equivalents balance (£3,556) in the financial statements of Baker Ltd. Materiality has been set at £4,000.

For each item select whether or not Lisa should test the item.

Current account balance (overdrawn) £5,600

A   Test

B   Not test

Petty cash float £750

C   Test

D   Not test

Special directors' cash account £1,294

E   Test

F   Not test   LO 3g

18 Kamran, an audit junior, has been asked to test the completeness of certain items in the income statement. He has carried out the following tests.

For each test carried out select whether that test proves the assertion of completeness or not.

Analytical procedures on revenue figures, budget v actual and actual current year v actual previous year

A   Proves completeness

B   Does not prove completeness

Tracing a sample of goods received notes to payables ledger and financial statements

C   Proves completeness

D   Does not prove completeness

Tracing a sample of entries on the payroll to individual HR records

E   Proves completeness

F   Does not prove completeness   LO 3d

19 Which TWO of the following assertions is the auditor most concerned with when testing property, plant and equipment?

A   Occurrence

B   Existence

C   Classification

D   Rights and obligations

E   Accuracy   LO 3d

20 The auditor of Mondays Ltd is performing a test to ensure that there are no omissions from the non-current asset register.

In respect of which of the following assertions will this procedure provide audit evidence?

A   Cut-off

B   Valuation

C   Completeness

D   Existence

E   Classification   LO 3d

21 Which TWO of the following procedures would provide evidence of rights and obligations of motor vehicles?

A   Vouching a sample of motor vehicles in the asset register to registration documents

B   Physical inspection of motor vehicles

C   Review of purchase invoices for motor vehicles acquired in the period

D   Confirmation that calculations on the non-current asset schedule are correct in respect of motor vehicles   LO 3d

22 For each of the following circumstances in respect of inventory, select which financial statement assertion would be affected.

Inventory which had been sold by the end of the period has been included in inventory

A   Completeness

B   Valuation

C   Cut-off

Damaged items of inventory have not been written down to net realisable value

D   Completeness

E   Valuation

F   Cut-off   LO 3d

23 For each of the following circumstances in respect of inventory, select which financial statement assertion would be affected.

Inventory items were excluded from the total in the financial statements in error

A   Completeness

B   Valuation

C   Cut-off

Due to the miscalculation of cost, some inventory items have been included at cost when net realisable value is lower

D   Completeness

E   Valuation

F   Cut-off   LO 3d

24 The following describes a number of features of the inventory count instructions of Sydney Ltd.

For each feature select whether it represents a strength or a deficiency.

The inventory count is performed by warehouse staff and supervised by the warehouse manager

A   Strength

B   Deficiency

Inventory sheets are completed in pencil

C   Strength

D   Deficiency

There are two teams of counters, one counting and one checking

E   Strength

F   Deficiency   LO 3g

25 For each of the following statements concerning perpetual inventory counts select whether they are true or false.

Adequate inventory records must be kept up to date

A   True

B   False

All inventory lines must be counted at least once per month

C   True

D   False

Material differences between book inventory and actual inventory must be investigated and corrected

E   True

F   False   LO 3g

26 Management should compare cost and net realisable value for each item of inventory.

Which THREE of the following circumstances could result in net realisable value being lower than cost?

A   An increase in the cost of raw materials which cannot be passed on to the customer

B   An increase in selling price

C   Errors in production

D   An increase in production overheads

E   Trade discounts from suppliers   LO 3g

27 Direct confirmation of trade receivables provides evidence in respect of which TWO of the following assertions?

   A   Existence

   B   Valuation

   C   Rights and obligations

   D   Completeness

   E   Occurrence   LO 3d

28 The following statements apply to the use of the positive or negative method of direct confirmation of receivables.

   For each statement, select whether it applies to a situation where the positive method should be used or to a situation where the negative method could be used.

   The assessed risk of material misstatement is high

   A   Positive method

   B   Negative method

   A small number of large balances is involved

   C   Positive method

   D   Negative method

   A substantial number of misstatements is not expected

   E   Positive method

   F   Negative method

   There is no reason to believe that respondents will disregard the requests

   G   Positive method

   H   Negative method   LO 3d

29 Which of the following is the MOST RELIABLE evidence of the valuation of trade receivables?

   A   A comparison of current year-end total with previous year

   B   Analysis of after-date receipts

   C   Reconciliation of receivables ledger and receivables ledger control account

   D   Reconstruction of receivables balance by tracing individual amounts invoiced to despatch notes

                                                                                      LO 3e

30   Smith and Co is considering the preliminary audit strategy for the following two new audit clients whose principal characteristics are set out below.

For each client, select whether Smith and Co would be likely to rely on internal controls or to rely completely on substantive procedures.

Client A has recently been incorporated and is experiencing rapid growth. It is in the process of recruiting a financial controller

A   Rely on internal controls

B   Rely completely on substantive procedures

Client B is an established company with well-documented systems and controls. It has an internal audit function whose principal activity is to monitor the implementation and effectiveness of existing controls

C   Rely on internal controls

D   Rely completely on substantive procedures   LO 3f

31   Two types of procedures used in gathering evidence are tests of controls and substantive procedures.

For each of the following examples select the type of procedure illustrated.

Examining the instructions issued by an organisation for its year-end physical inventory count

A   Test of control

B   Substantive procedure

Observing an organisation's despatch procedures

C   Test of control

D   Substantive procedure

Comparing this year's sales figures to those of previous years

E   Test of control

F   Substantive procedure   LO 3b

32   The following are examples of tests which an assurance firm might use at the gathering evidence stage of an assignment.

For each example select the type of procedure which that test illustrates.

Casting the list of year-end receivables

A   Confirmation

B   Recalculation

C   Reperformance

Using CAATs to check the ageing of the year-end list of aged receivables

D   Confirmation

E   Recalculation

F   Reperformance   LO 3b

33 In order to gather sufficient, appropriate evidence, the auditor may make use of external confirmation requests.

For each of the following statements with regards to external confirmation requests select whether it is true or false.

A positive confirmation request always asks the respondents to reply to the auditor indicating whether or not they agree with the information provided

A True

B False

A sample of confirmation requests drawn from the client's list of balances is more appropriate for receivables balances than for payables balances

C True

D False

A positive confirmation request ordinarily provides more reliable audit evidence than a negative confirmation request

E True

F False   LO 3c

34 Which of the following financial statement assertions will be supported by a sample check on the numerical sequence of despatch notes and invoices?

A Allocation

B Occurrence

C Completeness

D Valuation   LO 3d

35 Which of the following procedures should be undertaken to confirm the existence of cash at bank?

A Inspecting the bank reconciliation statement prepared by the client

B Agreeing the figures on the bank reconciliation to the bank column in the cash book

C Obtaining direct confirmation of the bank balance from the client's bank

D Reperforming the additions on the bank reconciliation   LO 3d

36   The auditor of Raindrop Ltd carried out a receivables circularisation at the year end to confirm the accuracy of total trade receivables in the statement of financial position at that date. Two of the replies to the circularisation disagreed the balance.

For each of these two disagreements select whether the disagreement would be considered a misstatement for the purpose of evaluating the accuracy of total trade receivables in the statement of financial position at the year end.

Jones and Co disagreed the balance because their records indicated that the amount had been paid a few days before the year end. The auditor's enquiries revealed that the cheque was cleared shortly after the year end

A   Misstatement

B   Not misstatement

Sunny plc disagreed the balance because its records indicated that it had paid the balance two weeks prior to the year end. The auditor's enquiries revealed that the amount had been received and credited to another customer's account prior to the year end

C   Misstatement

D   Not misstatement   LO 3g

37   The external auditor of Aaron Ltd has set materiality thresholds such that items under £40,000 are not generally considered material.

For each of the following items in Aaron Ltd's financial statements select whether the auditor would test it primarily for overstatement or primarily for understatement, or whether the item would not be tested at all.

£1,000 due from Harry, a director of Aaron Ltd

A   Overstatement

B   Understatement

C   Not test

Sundry income £35,000

D   Overstatement

E   Understatement

F   Not test   LO 3f/g

38   Gamma Ltd has a head office and several branches. The head office operates a continuous inventory counting system which ensures that all items are counted at least twice a year and checked against inventory records.

During the interim audit, an examination of the counts undertaken by head office staff shows that differences between inventory records and the physical count regularly arise. Usually, actual inventory levels at branches are found to be higher than book inventory.

Which of the following explains this difference?

A   Unrecorded write offs of scrapped inventory

B   Unrecorded purchase returns

C   Unrecorded branch requisitions

D   Unrecorded branch returns   LO 3g

39 The results of assigned substantive audit tests at Errata plc are set out below. The materiality threshold set for these tests was £1,000.

For each of the following results select the action which should be taken by the audit senior.

No misstatements found

A   Draw conclusion

B   Refer to senior colleague

C   Extend sample

An arithmetical misstatement of £5,000 found

D   Draw conclusion

E   Refer to senior colleague

F   Extend sample

A misstatement of £10 found, sanctioned by the finance director

G   Draw conclusion

H   Refer to senior colleague

I   Extend sample   LO 3i

---

40 Which of the following describes how an assurance provider would check the existence assertion for a non-current asset?

A   Trace the physical item to the non-current asset register

B   Trace the physical item to the financial statements

C   Trace an entry in the non-current asset register to the physical item

D   Trace an entry in the non-current asset register to the financial statements

E   Trace an entry in the financial statements to the physical item   LO 3f

Chapter 14: Codes of professional ethics

1   Which THREE of the following are reasons why the accounting profession needs ethical codes?

   A   Accountants have access to confidential information

   B   Assurance providers claim to give an independent view

   C   The financial community relies on accountants

   D   The law requires it   LO 4a/c/l

2   ICAEW qualified auditors acting in the UK are subject to which TWO of the following?

   A   IFAC Code of Ethics

   B   ICAEW Code of Ethics

   C   FRC's Ethical Standards for Auditors

   D   The Code of Ethics set by the Government   LO 4d

3   Which THREE of the following are stated fundamental principles of the IFAC Code?

   A   Integrity

   B   Objectivity

   C   Independence

   D   Confidentiality

   E   Courtesy   LO 4e

4   Which of the following statements is correct?

   A   The ICAEW Code of Ethics applies to its members only

   B   The ICAEW Code of Ethics applies to its members and employees of member firms only

   C   The ICAEW Code of Ethics applies to its members, employees of member firms and ICAEW students

   D   The ICAEW Code of Ethics applies to its members, employees of member firms, ICAEW students and all other members of UK accountancy bodies   LO 4d

5   For each of the following statements concerning professional ethics select whether they are true or false.

Prescriptive rules of ethical guidance are beneficial because they place the onus on the accountant to actively consider independence in every given situation

A   True

B   False

A framework of ethical guidance allows principles to be applied to different situations and is therefore effective in a situation that is changing rapidly

C   True

D   False

A framework of ethical guidance prevents accountants interpreting legalistic requirements narrowly in order to circumvent ethical requirements

E   True

F   False   LO 4b

6   Which THREE of the following bodies issue ethical guidance?

A   ICAEW

B   IFAC

C   IAASB

D   FRC   LO 4d

7   Which of the following statements best describes ethical guidance in the UK?

A   Ethical guidance provides a set of rules which must be followed in all circumstances

B   Ethical guidance is a framework containing a combination of rules and principles the application of which is dependent on the professional judgement of the assurance provider based on the specific circumstances

C   Ethical guidance provides a set of principles which can be applied at the discretion of the assurance provider

D   Ethical guidance is a series of legal requirements   LO 4d

8   For each of the following threats select whether they are identified by the IFAC Code only, the FRC's Ethical Standards for Auditors only or both the IFAC Code and the FRC Ethical Standards for Auditors.

Self-interest threat

A   IFAC Code only

B   FRC Ethical Standards for Auditors only

C   Both

Management threat

D   IFAC Code only

E   FRC Ethical Standards for Auditors only

F   Both

Familiarity threat

G   IFAC Code only

H   FRC Ethical Standards for Auditors only

I   Both

Self-review threat

J   IFAC Code only

K   FRC Ethical Standards for Auditors only

L   Both   LO 4f

9   Which THREE of the following are valid reasons why independence and objectivity are important to the assurance profession?

A   The public's expectations of accountants

B   Public interest in financial information

C   Tradition

D   Credibility of published financial information   LO 4f

10   There are two main approaches to a code of professional ethics: a rules-based ethical code and a code based upon a set of principles.

Indicate whether the following statements are true or false.

A code based upon a set of principles requires a professional accountant to comply with a set of specific rules

A   True

B   False

A rules-based code requires a professional accountant to identify, evaluate and address threats to compliance with fundamental ethical principles

C   True

D   False

The ICAEW uses a rules-based approach

E   True

F   False   LO 4b/d

Chapter 15: Integrity, objectivity and independence

1   Which THREE of the following should an auditor consider if there is a threat to independence?

    A   Withdrawing from the engagement

    B   Applying specific safeguards

    C   Making disclosures to the client

    D   Making disclosures to the ICAEW   LO 4g

2   Which THREE of the following should not own a material financial interest in an audit client?

    A   A member of the audit team

    B   A minor child of a member of the audit team

    C   A parent of a member of the audit team

    D   A spouse of a member of the audit team   LO 4f

3   Which THREE of the following threats to independence might arise on the current audit when an audit team member is involved in employment negotiations with an audit client during the course of the audit?

    A   Self-interest

    B   Self-review

    C   Intimidation

    D   Familiarity   LO 4m

4   Allisons and Co is a firm of Chartered Accountants. It has a reputation for excellence in the banking and insurance industry and has been invited to accept engagements by various institutions as follows.

    (i)   The audit of Nationally plc, the leading building society in the UK. 40% of staff members of Allisons and Co who have mortgages have mortgaged their home with Nationally.

    (ii)   The audit of Cash It Ltd, a large business which banks cheques and cash items for the general public and also advances loans. A member of the proposed audit team was impressed by the loan rate offered to the team during the tendering process and took out a loan with Cash It Ltd to buy a car.

    Which, if any, of the above companies present a major threat to the independence of Allisons and Co, if the engagement were to be accepted?

    A   Nationally plc and Cash It Ltd

    B   Cash It Ltd only

    C   Nationally plc only

    D   Neither Nationally plc nor Cash It Ltd   LO 4f

5   Which of the following is correct in relation to the presumption of dependence for a non-listed client?

    A   There is a presumption of dependence when annual fee income from all services to the client will regularly exceed 15% of gross practice income

    B   There is a presumption of dependence when annual fee income from all services to the client will regularly exceed 5% of gross practice income

    C   There is a presumption of dependence when annual assurance fee income from all services to the client will regularly exceed 15% of gross practice income

    D   There is a presumption of dependence when annual assurance fee income from all services to the client will regularly exceed 5% of gross practice income   LO 4f

6   Majors and Co, a firm of Chartered Accountants, offers the following additional services to various audit clients.

In which THREE of the following situations is an insurmountable self-review threat most likely to arise?

    A   Preparing the financial statements for Power Group plc, a listed company, on a regular basis

    B   Carrying out valuations of various non-current property assets for Tower Investments Ltd, a property investment company

    C   Promoting tax structures to Haven Ltd, where there is scope for doubt about the appropriateness of the accounting treatments involved to achieve the tax benefits

    D   Assisting Craven plc in defining its corporate strategies and identifying possible sources of finance for a potential new venture   LO 4f

7   In accordance with Ethical Standard 3, in which THREE of the following engagements is there a significant threat to independence?

    A   Alan Johnson has been the audit engagement partner of Domino Ltd for eleven years

    B   Barry Thomson has been the audit engagement partner of Beetle Group plc, a listed company, for seven years

    C   Having been the audit engagement partner of Risk Group plc, a listed company, for five years, Colin Jackson resigned as audit engagement partner three years ago. Following a reshuffle in the firm, he has just been assigned as a key partner involved in the audit of Risk Group plc

    D   Don Matthewson has recently been appointed as the audit engagement partner of Scrabble plc, a listed company. He previously held this position six years ago   LO 4f

8   The ethics partner at Juleyson Co, a firm of Chartered Accountants, is trying to resolve an ethical conflict in respect of two clients of the firm.

Which TWO of the following are appropriate actions for him to take?

    A   Do nothing because the situation is likely to resolve itself over time

    B   Refer the matter to the management board of partners because he cannot determine a solution himself

    C   Solicit advice from the ICAEW ethics helpline

    D   Seek the opinion of an ethics partner at a different firm   LO 4o

9   Julia is a member of the ICAEW who works in industry at KiwiCorp plc, a listed company. The company is experiencing difficulty meeting the expectations of the market, and Julia has been told by the board of directors that the company must meet its optimistic profit targets at the year end, regardless of what accounting is required to achieve this.

Which TWO of the following are the MOST APPROPRIATE initial courses of action for Julia to take in these circumstances?

A   Report her concerns to the audit committee

B   Resign

C   Take legal advice

D   Obtain advice from the human resources department at KiwiCorp plc   LO 4o

10 Threats to independence can be placed into six general categories of threat.

For each of the following statements select whether they are true or false.

Having a close business relationship, including a common financial interest with an audit client, can cause self-interest and intimidation threats

A   True

B   False

A partner should not serve on an audit client's board as this can constitute a management threat

C   True

D   False

Contingent fees for audit work cause a self-interest threat

E   True

F   False   LO 4m

11 There are various general threats to independence recognised by ethical codes.

For the following two examples, select a type of threat which might arise in that situation.

The audit senior assigned to the audit of Loesdon Ltd has recently become engaged to the finance director's daughter

A   Self-interest

B   Management

C   Advocacy

The finance director of Litten Ltd has recently informed the audit engagement partner that Litten Ltd will be seeking a stock exchange listing. The finance director has implied that Litten Ltd will want to use the firm for significant amounts of advisory work in relation to the listing, but joked at the same time that 'clean bills of health' would be crucial from now on

D   Self-interest

E   Management

F   Self-review   LO 4m

12 Estelle and Co is a ten-partner assurance firm which has been asked to consider taking on the audit of the financial statements of two separate companies. The following potential issues have been identified prior to acceptance of any such appointments.

For each of the following clients select the basis on which the engagement could be accepted, if at all.

Othello Ltd, which will also require you to provide routine tax compliance work and advice

A   Do not accept

B   Accept with safeguards

C   Accept with no safeguards

Desdemona Ltd, the finance director of which worked at Estelle and Co four years ago, but who does not know any of the members of the proposed audit team personally

D   Do not accept

E   Accept with safeguards

F   Accept with no safeguards   LO 4g

---

13 Fagin and Co, a large assurance firm, has been asked to carry out recruitment services for its client, Claret plc, by recruiting senior accounting staff.

Which TWO of the following threats to independence would arise if Fagin and Co agree to provide such services?

A   Self-review

B   Management

C   Advocacy

D   Familiarity   LO 4m

---

14 The following are examples of situations in which an audit firm might be faced with threats to its independence.

For each example, select the type of threat which that situation BEST illustrates.

The finance director of Fussy Ltd has requested that the audit team for the current year audit be the same as the team which performed last year's audit

A   Self-review

B   Familiarity

C   Intimidation

The finance director of Pernickety Ltd has told the audit manager that he is not happy with the proposed audit opinion and is likely to seek a second opinion

D   Self-review

E   Familiarity

F   Intimidation   LO 4m

15   The following are examples of situations in which Carnation and Co, an audit firm with 50 similar medium-sized audit clients, which are non-listed, might need to implement safeguards in order to protect its independence.

For each situation select the most appropriate safeguard or state that there are no safeguards that could reduce the risk to an appropriate level.

Carnation and Co has been invited to accept the audit of a major listed company. The fee income from this engagement would represent 5% of the gross fee income of the firm

A   Separate personnel

B   Discuss the issues with the audit committee

C   No safeguards possible

Carnation and Co has been invited to accept the audit of a major competitor of an existing client and has obtained consent from both to act

D   Separate personnel

E   Discuss the issues with the audit committee

F   No safeguards possible

LO 4n

16   Hermione and Co is a twelve-partner assurance firm which has been asked to consider taking on the statutory audit of two separate companies. The following potential issues have been identified prior to acceptance of any such appointments.

For each of the following potential clients select on what basis the engagement could be accepted, if at all.

Snowman Ltd, which has just grown to the point where a statutory audit is required. Snowman Ltd is already a client of Hermione and Co, which prepares the financial statements for the company

A   Do not accept

B   Accept with safeguards

C   Accept with no safeguards

Snowball Ltd, which is a competitor of an existing client of Hermione and Co

D   Do not accept

E   Accept with safeguards

F   Accept with no safeguards

LO 4g

17   Which THREE of the following are areas in which a self-interest threat might arise?

A   Where there is a close business relationship between the auditor and the client

B   Where the auditor prepares and audits the financial statements

C   Where the auditor has a financial interest in the client

D   Where there are a significant amount of overdue fees

E   Where the audit firm provides internal audit services and significant reliance is to be placed on the internal audit work for the purposes of the external audit

LO 4m

18 Monty and Co, an audit firm, has a number of medium-sized audit clients which are non-listed. It has a current gross practice income of £500,000.

For each of the following prospective clients taken separately, select whether there are safeguards which could reduce any risk to independence to an acceptable level.

Marty Ltd has insisted that the audit fee be based on 5% of reported profit after tax

A   Safeguards possible

B   No safeguards possible

Fee income in respect of Andrews Ltd is expected to be £95,000

C   Safeguards possible

D   No safeguards possible

Fee income in respect of Borne Ltd is expected to be £65,000

E   Safeguards possible

F   No safeguards possible   LO 4f

19 Wright and Co, a firm of auditors, has the following employees who previously worked for current audit clients.

Name	Previous employer	Position held	Date of resignation
Sam Brown	Hastle Ltd	Finance director	31 January 20X6
James Sanderson	Hastle Ltd	Office junior	30 June 20X7
Sally Jones	Morgan Ltd	Chief accountant	1 June 20X4

For the audit of Hastle Ltd and Morgan Ltd for the year ended 31 December 20X7 for which, if either, could all three members of staff be used on the audit team?

A   Both Hastle Ltd and Morgan Ltd

B   Hastle Ltd only

C   Morgan Ltd only

D   Neither Hastle Ltd nor Morgan Ltd   LO 4f

20 Edward is an audit trainee working on the audit of Trekker Trailers Ltd. It is the day before the audit manager is coming out to the client to review the files. Edward has been asked to perform some additional tests on inventory valuation by his supervisor. These tests have revealed a number of problems which Edward has highlighted to the supervisor. The supervisor has told Edward that it is too late to deal with these and has asked him to falsify the working papers.

Which of the following is the most appropriate course of action for Edward to take?

A   Falsify the results as instructed

B   Inform the audit manager

C   Seek legal advice

D   Inform the client   LO 4o

21 Morgan and Co, an audit firm, has a number of prospective clients: Masons Ltd, Burton Ltd and Dewburry Ltd.

For each of these following prospective clients select whether the holding of the stated financial interest should result in the firm declining the engagement or the individual being excluded from the audit team. (Assume that the interests are not disposed of).

Bill Brown, a partner in Morgan and Co, owns 10% of the shares in Masons Ltd.

A   Firm must decline

B   Individual excluded

Sam Larson's wife owns 5% of the shares in Burton Ltd. Sam Larson is an audit manager at Morgan and Co.

C   Firm must decline

D   Individual excluded

Jane Smith's husband owns 15% of the shares in Dewburry Ltd. Jane Smith is a partner in Morgan and Co.

E   Firm must decline

F   Individual excluded   LO 4f

22 The following are examples of situations in which Panama and Co, an audit firm with thirty similar medium-sized audit clients, which are non-listed, might need to implement safeguards in order to protect its independence.

For each situation select the most appropriate safeguard or state that there are no safeguards which could reduce the risk to an acceptable level.

One of Panama and Co's clients is a competitor of one of its other clients

A   Separate personnel

B   Fee threshold not exceeded

C   No safeguards possible

Panama and Co has been asked to take on the role of internal auditor at one of its clients and would be responsible for implementing its own recommendations

D   Separate personnel

E   Fee threshold not exceeded

F   No safeguards possible   LO 4n

23 Cairns and Co, a small assurance firm, has been asked to provide two of its audit clients with the following additional services. For each of the companies, select on what basis the additional services could be provided, if at all.

Leyton Ltd has had to employ a new accountant who is unsure of the correct treatment of a number of transactions. Cairns and Co has been asked to provide advice and assist in the preparation of the financial statements.

A   Do not provide

B   Provide with safeguards

C   Provide with no safeguards

Blacks Ltd has asked Cairns and Co to provide some tax planning advice and has suggested that the fee could be based on a percentage of the tax saving. The total fee from this client is material to Cairns and Co.

D   Do not provide

E   Provide with safeguards

F   Provide with no safeguards   LO 4g

24 In each of the following cases, select the principal threat that the audit firm is facing.

Polly Nunn, a partner in an audit firm, has just inherited some shares in an audit client

A   Self-interest

B   Familiarity

Golf World Ltd is so pleased with the way that the audit has been conducted that it has offered the members of the audit team two free golf lessons each

C   Self-interest

D   Familiarity

Tobin and Co, an audit firm, has been asked to provide internal audit services to an audit client

E   Self-interest

F   Self-review   LO 4m

25 Jane Stanley is a qualified accountant working for a small catering company. The directors of the company are looking to expand and have approached a number of potential investors. Jane has been asked to produce management accounts for the investors to review. The managing director has specifically told her that they must show a gross profit margin of 30% and he 'doesn't care how she achieves it'. The gross profit margin is normally approximately 20%. There is no internal complaints procedure.

Which of the following is the most appropriate INITIAL course of action for Jane to take?

A   Resign

B   Seek legal advice

C   Contact ICAEW telephone helpline

D   Comply with her employer's request   LO 4o

26 Richard Richardson and Co is a multi-national audit firm responsible for the audit of a high street bank, Barkers Bank.

For each example below of loans provided to members of the audit team by Barkers Bank select whether the loan gives rise to a threat to Richard Richardson and Co's independence.

The audit junior's student loan

A   Threat

B   No threat

The audit partner's mortgage, negotiated on normal commercial terms

C   Threat

D   No threat

The audit manager has recently taken out a car loan. He is being charged an interest rate of 2% below the standard rate applied to this product

E   Threat

F   No threat   LO 4f

27 The following are examples of situations in which an audit firm might be faced with threats to its independence.

For each example select the type of threat which that situation illustrates.

The audit firm has been asked to underwrite its client's shares in relation to a proposed flotation

A   Self-review

B   Advocacy

The board of directors does not contain a qualified finance professional and the company has asked the audit firm to prepare the financial statements

C   Self-review

D   Advocacy   LO 4m

28 Talland and Co is the external auditor of Huntley plc, a retailer. The managing partner has been called to a meeting with the board of directors of Huntley plc. At that meeting the firm has been asked if it can provide the following non-audit services.

Huntley plc wish to implement a new sales system. They wish Talland and Co to take on a consultancy project whereby the firm will evaluate several possible systems, advise on which system should be selected, and oversee the installation of the new system.

Which of the following sets of threats would arise from the above scenario, if the project was accepted by Talland and Co?

A   Advocacy and management

B   Management and familiarity

C   Management and self-review

D   Advocacy and familiarity   LO 4m

29 Hammers and Co is a firm of Chartered Accountants. It has been invited to accept engagements by various institutions as follows.

    (i)   Advisers to New Generation Insurance and Co, a small group of insurers seeking to buy out the home insurance business of Insurance Plus, a major UK insurer. The partner in charge of the advice team has made certain guarantees to New Generation Insurance and Co's bank in respect of one of the members of New Generation Insurance and Co, whom he knows personally. Hammers and Co has been promised the audit of New Generation Insurance and Co if the buy out is successful.

    (ii)   A review of banking procedures at NatEast plc, a major high street bank. Hammers and Co has a modest business loan from NatEast plc.

Which, if any, of the above companies presents a major threat to the independence of Hammers and Co, if the engagement were to be accepted?

    A   New Generation Insurance and Co and NatEast plc

    B   NatEast plc only

    C   New Generation Insurance and Co only

    D   Neither New Generation Insurance and Co nor NatEast plc   LO 4f

---

30 The following are examples of situations in which Bouldry and Co, an audit firm, might need to implement safeguards to protect its independence. Bouldry and Co has 75 small, non-listed audit clients and has been asked to provide additional services to three of these clients.

For each situation select whether the additional services could be accepted with appropriate safeguards or state that there are no safeguards that could reduce the risk to an appropriate level.

Bouldry and Co has been asked to carry out a valuation service. The valuation is material to the financial statements but does not involve a significant degree of subjectivity

    A   Accept with safeguards

    B   No safeguards possible

Bouldry and Co has been asked to provide accounts preparation assistance

    C   Accept with safeguards

    D   No safeguards possible

Bouldry and Co has been asked to design and implement an IT system which will significantly impact on the accounting system. Historically, Bouldry and Co has placed reliance on the accounting system as part of the audit.

    E   Accept with safeguards

    F   No safeguards possible   LO 4g

---

31 Brown & Co has been invited by Alpha plc, a listed company, and Beta Ltd , a non-listed company, to provide audit and non-audit services. If accepted, the fees would represent in the case of Alpha plc 11% and in the case of Beta Ltd 12% of the gross fee income of the firm.

Assuming Brown & Co wishes to take on as many clients as is permitted by Ethical Standards, which of the following is the most appropriate course of action?

    A   Accept both Alpha plc and Beta Ltd as clients

    B   Accept Alpha plc as a client and refuse Beta Ltd

    C   Accept Beta Ltd as a client and refuse Alpha plc

    D   Refuse to take on either Alpha plc or Beta Ltd as clients   LO 4f

---

32   Helena and Co is an eight-partner assurance firm which has been asked to consider taking on the statutory audit of two separate companies. The following potential issues have been identified prior to acceptance of any such appointments.

For each of the following potential clients select on what basis the engagement could be accepted, if at all.

Titania plc, a listed company, which will also require you to prepare the financial statements

A   Do not accept

B   Accept with safeguards

C   Accept with no safeguards

Puck Ltd, whose finance director is the brother of one of the partners at the assurance firm

D   Do not accept

E   Accept with safeguards

F   Accept with no safeguards   LO 4g

33   Two different audit juniors have been asked to carry out the following tasks. In each case you should select the action that the audit junior should take.

An audit junior at Oberon and Co, a large assurance firm, has been asked to join the audit team at a major client to carry out the receivables section of the audit. The junior has not carried out this section of the audit before but has covered it in his training

A   Perform the work

B   Refer to training partner

C   Contact ICAEW telephone helpline

An audit junior at Lear and Co, a sole practitioner audit firm, has been asked to commence the audit of a small manufacturing client. The junior has expressed reservation about this but the practitioner has insisted that he should go out to the client unsupervised at the beginning of the following week

D   Perform the work

E   Refer to training partner

F   Contact ICAEW telephone helpline   LO 4h

34   David, a recently qualified chartered accountant, is the newly-appointed financial controller of Hartpury Ltd. Hartpury Ltd is a relatively small company, which is ripe for takeover.

As one of his first assignments, David has been asked to prepare the financial statements for the year ended 31 December 20X6. David has now been called into the last part of a board meeting where the directors have given him a profit target which must be met in those financial statements. They have stressed that this profit target must be met, even if it means that accounting standards are not followed.

Which TWO of the following describe possible appropriate courses of action which David could consider taking?

A   Report his concerns to the audit committee

B   Resign his post

C   Report his concerns to the finance director

D   Take legal advice

E   Use Hartpury Ltd's formal dispute resolution process to resolve the issue   LO 4o

35   The following are examples of situations in which an audit firm might be faced with threats to its independence.

For each example select the principal type of threat which that situation illustrates.

The finance director has a very strong personality and insists on the audit team working in his office

A   Familiarity

B   Intimidation

C   Management

The audit team and the management team at the client have remained unchanged for several years

D   Familiarity

E   Intimidation

F   Management   LO 4m

36   Dudley & Partners is a large assurance firm. They have acted as the external auditors to Birmingham Ltd, a small owner-managed company, for two years.

The managing director and major shareholder of Birmingham Ltd, Mr Black, has now asked the firm to represent the company's interests in a legal case which has been brought against it. Mr Black has indicated that if the firm refuse to do this they will not be reappointed as external auditor. He is also making matters difficult for those members of the audit team carrying out the interim audit.

Which of the following sets of threats arises from the above scenario?

A   Intimidation, self-review and management

B   Advocacy, self-interest and management

C   Intimidation, advocacy and self-interest

D   Intimidation, advocacy and management   LO 4m

1 Which TWO of the following are the principal reasons why confidentiality is so important to accountants?

    A   It is a fundamental principle of all the major ethical codes

    B   Failure to keep information confidential reflects badly on the accountant

    C   Accountants need their clients to be comfortable to make full disclosure of company affairs to them

    D   It means that accountants can work for competitors   LO 4i

2 Which THREE of the following should an accountant take care not to do, in order to safeguard confidentiality?

    A   Discuss client matters with third parties

    B   Discuss client matters with colleagues in public places

    C   Discuss client matters with colleagues in non-public places

    D   Leave working papers in the car   LO 4j

3 In which THREE of the following situations is it appropriate to disclose confidential information?

    A   When the client has granted permission

    B   In order to obtain audit evidence about an amount in the financial statements

    C   When there is a public duty to make disclosure

    D   When there is a legal duty to make disclosure   LO 4k

4 Which THREE of the following are situations where there is a legal duty to disclose confidential information?

    A   When a fraud has taken place, it should be reported to the police

    B   When terrorist activity has taken place, it should be reported to the police

    C   When regulatory breaches have taken place at a charity, it should be reported to the Charities Commission

    D   When money laundering is suspected, it should be reported to the Serious Organised Crime Agency (SOCA)   LO 4k

5   Emma is faced with the following situations as part of her work.

For each situation select the action Emma should take.

As part of her routine assurance work on revenue at Dodgy Ltd, Emma discovers that the company accepts cash payments for sales that are never recorded in the accounting records

A   Make no external report

B   Report to the police

C   Report to the firm's money laundering reporting officer

As part of her routine payables testing at Risky Ltd, Emma discovers that controls are deficient and some payments have been made to suppliers twice in error

D   Make no external report

E   Report to the police

F   Report to the firm's money laundering reporting officer   LO 4k

6   For each of the following situations select whether the assurance provider MAY disclose confidential information or MUST disclose confidential information.

The assurance provider is being sued for negligence and is trying to establish a defence

A   May make disclosure

B   Must make disclosure

The assurance provider has discovered a fraud at the client, which the client has agreed should be referred to the police

C   May make disclosure

D   Must make disclosure

The assurance provider believes that the client is saving money by breaching environmental clean up requirements

E   May make disclosure

F   Must make disclosure   LO 4k

7   In which of the following instances would the client's permission be required before disclosure is made to a third party?

A   The client is involved in tax evasion

B   The receivables ledger clerk at a client has committed a theft by teeming and lading

C   An employee of a client is involved in terrorist activities

D   The client, in order to save costs, has failed to apply for a licence to operate which is required by law   LO 4k

8   If an assurance provider suspects that money laundering is taking place to which of the following should the details be reported in the first instance?

A   The police

B   The Department of Trade and Industry

C   The board of directors

D   The firm's money laundering reporting officer   LO 4k

9   In respect of conflicts of interest select whether each of the following statements is true or false.

Where a conflict of interest exists between two audit clients the auditor must cease to act for one party

A   True

B   False

If the effects of a conflict of interest can be mitigated by safeguards these should be recorded

C   True

D   False

Where adequate safeguards are available the parties involved do not need to be informed of the conflict of interest

E   True

F   False   LO 4n

10 Which TWO of the following would be an APPROPRIATE use of confidential information?

A   On a change of employment, using experience gained in a previous position

B   Encouraging others to buy shares in a company on the basis of information obtained during the course of the audit

C   Providing a prospective auditor with information required by him in order for him to decide whether or not to accept the appointment

D   Using information obtained on the audit of one client to influence the audit opinion given in respect of another client   LO 4k

11 In which of the following situations may confidential information in respect of a client ONLY be disclosed if the permission of the client has first been granted?

A   As a defence in a negligence claim

B   In order to avoid giving an incorrect audit report to another client

C   Where money laundering is suspected

D   Where terrorism is suspected   LO 4k

12 During the course of an assurance engagement, a member of the assurance team from Endeavour and Co discovers that the owner of the business regularly collects cash received from customers and does not include any details relating to the transaction in the accounting records of the business.

Which of the following is the most appropriate action for him to take in respect of this matter?

A   Discuss the matter with the client and advise him of the legal position

B   Report the matter to the manager of the assurance engagement so that she can discuss it with the client

C   Obtain the client's permission to report the matter to a designated officer within your firm

D   Report the matter to a designated officer within your firm without the client's permission LO 4k

Answer Bank

Chapter 1: Concept of and need for assurance

1   A,B,C

A key element of an assurance engagement is sufficient appropriate evidence, but is not generally mandatory that this evidence is recorded in an assurance file. (It is mandatory to record audit evidence, however.)

2   A,B,D

Reasonable assurance is a high, *but not absolute,* level of assurance. The other options available represent various aspects of the expectations gap which is the gap between what the assurance provider understands he is doing and what the user of the information believes he is doing.

3   D   Employment by a firm controlled by qualified persons. Membership of a recognised supervisory body cannot be obtained until exams have been passed, but provided that the person is employed by a qualifying person/firm, work can be carried out on audits.

4   B,C   The answer is not option A as the fact that assurance work is carried out by independent people is a strength of assurance provision. Option D is also incorrect as the use of unqualified staff increases the detection risk of the auditor as opposed to being an inherent limitation of the provision of assurance. Work carried out by less qualified staff should always be supervised, directed and reviewed by more senior personnel.

5   C,E   It is the responsible party who will determine the suitable criteria (in response to the obligations it has) against which the practitioner will test the subject matter and on which the practitioner will report to the users.

It is the practitioner who will provide the opinion on whether the subject matter complies with the criteria after the evidence has been gathered and evaluated accordingly. The opinion prepared will be issued to the user.

6   B   Sufficient appropriate audit evidence is gathered and a positive opinion issued in a reasonable assurance engagement. A lower level of evidence coupled with a negative opinion applies to a limited assurance engagement.

7   A,C,F

Whereas the statutory audit provides reasonable assurance through a positive assurance conclusion, in a review engagement, limited assurance is provided with the issue of the negative assurance conclusion. This can be seen in the wording of the two conclusions. The positive assurance conclusion includes wording "the financial statements give a true and fair view", whereas the negative assurance conclusion includes the wording "nothing has come to our attention", emphasising the limited nature of the assignment.

Reasonable assurance is high assurance provided on the truth and fairness of the subject matter as opposed to absolute assurance of the correctness of the subject matter.

8   A,D,F

The subject matter under examination are the company's corporate governance policies. These policies are to be assessed against the UK Corporate Governance Code, which is the suitable criteria. The responsible party is Blue plc, the party commissioning the report, who has the responsibility to apply the UK Corporate Governance Code. Jones & Co is the practitioner, responsible for gathering the appropriate evidence and issuing an appropriate opinion.

9   B,D,E

Criteria used will depend on the type of engagement conducted. Suitable criteria should be available for other engagements eg health and safety can be measured against health and safety legislation.

10 A,D Reasonable assurance engagements include the statutory audit. The auditor's report is phrased positively but does not give absolute assurance. Negative assurance indicates that nothing has come to light which would cast doubt on the subject matter being reviewed.

11 A,C As per Companies Act, 2006, a statutory auditor must be a member of a recognised supervisory body and an officer or employee of the client is ineligible as auditor.

12 B Assurance refers to an assurance firm's satisfaction as to the reliability of an assertion being made by one party for the use of another party. This assurance is then expressed in an assurance report with a negative or positive conclusion given as appropriate to that particular engagement.

13 C An assurance report does not 'attest(s) to the correctness of the information being reported upon'. Even a reasonable assurance engagement (which gives more assurance than a limited assurance engagement) does not provide a guarantee that the information being reported on is correct. Assurance can never be absolute as this statement implies.

14 A,E It is the responsible party that prepares the subject matter and the practitioner who is responsible for gathering evidence. The user is the party who receives the final report.

15 D There are two types of conclusion which can be given: a conclusion expressed in positive terms and a conclusion expressed in negative terms. A conclusion expressed in negative terms is indicated by the phrase 'nothing has come to our attention' which indicates the restricted work carried out and hence the fact that the assurance is limited, as opposed to reasonable. Hence this type of assurance is limited level of assurance expressed negatively.

16 A,B,D

The expectation gap is the gap between what users of financial statements believe the auditor does and what the auditor actually does. The following three are common manifestations of the expectation gap:

- The auditor's report certifies the financial statements as correct
- The auditor's principal duty is to detect fraud
- The auditor checks all transactions.

The belief that the auditor is employed by the directors is a common misconception but not a manifestation of the expectation gap. (The company employs the auditor, who is appointed by the shareholders in a general meeting.)

17 B,D,F

A statutory audit provides reasonable assurance, which reflects the comprehensiveness of the audit procedures carried out. No assurance engagement, not even a statutory audit can give absolute assurance.

1   A,B   The answer is not option C as it will not be necessary to obtain references when the entity is already known to the firm. It will not be necessary to contact previous auditors in the case of a company's first audit.

2   A,C   Poor recent performance may indicate a high risk that the company may misstate its financial statements in order to show improved recent performance. A company carrying out unusual transactions would also be a high risk, as each transaction would require a separate understanding leading to a higher risk of error. Strong internal controls and the existence of an internal audit department would be low risk indicators.

3   A,C   Given its intention to list on the stock exchange, Tulip Ltd may be motivated to show a better picture of itself than that which exists, hence it is a high risk client. Dhalia Ltd is also a high risk client given that it is seeking alternative forms of finance. It has the incentive to show itself as a more healthy company than it actually is in order to attract the finance it requires.

4   D   The engagement letter does not contain any certification of the assurance provider's opinion. An engagement letter does serve the other purposes listed.

5   B,C,E

Prudent accounting policies would constitute a low risk indicator as directors would appear not to be aggressive in interpreting accounting policies in order to enhance the performance portrayed by the financial statements.

A company carrying out unusual transactions would be high risk, as each transaction would require a separate understanding leading to a higher risk of error.

Having no FD is a high risk indicator – the staff in the function may not be supervised and they may not have the skills or the knowledge to apply accounting standards and address the key risks in the systems of the company.

6   C,E   It is the letter of engagement that clarifies the terms of the engagement and initial communication that requests for relevant information pertaining to acceptance of the engagement. The tender proposal would come before these two stages at the audit tender process stage.

7   A,B,D

Checks on legal and ethical restrictions should be performed BEFORE the appointment is accepted. Once the appointment is accepted, legal and professional obligations need to addressed, options A and B (as per Companies Act 2006) and option D as per ISA 210 *Agreeing the Terms of Audit Engagements*.

8   B,C,F,G

The engagement letter is essentially the contract between the client and the auditor and therefore should be sent to all clients. It confirms acceptance of the appointment by the auditor so must be issued after acceptance but before work is commenced.

9   A   Money Laundering Regulations 2007 state that client identification documents must be kept for a minimum of five years and until five years since the relationship elapses.

10   A,C   Arrangements regarding the planning and performance and the basis of the fee calculation are not essential to be included in the engagement letter, whereas the responsibilities of the auditor and the form of any reports must be included in the engagement letter.

11 A,C,D

The following are not purposes of an engagement letter:

- Providing constructive suggestions to management concerning improvements to internal control

- Providing evidence on matters where other evidence is not expected to exist (eg on management plans for the future of the entity) – this is the purpose of a written representation.

12 C   Apply a questioning mind to the information and evidence he obtains would indicate professional scepticism. The alternative options offered are all a step too far.

1   B,C,D

   The answer is not option A as to determine the scope of the engagement should have been done in the engagement letter.

2   A,C,D

   The standard states that inquiries of third parties MAY be carried out if useful, but lists options A, C and D as procedures that SHALL be carried out.

3   A,B,D

   The answer is not option C as consideration of whether a balance has been correctly calculated will require a procedure of recalculation as opposed to analytical procedure.

4   A   What audit staff to assign to the audit (this would depend more on the risks associated with the engagement).

5   A,B,D

   Option C is incorrect as confirmation of management's responsibility for the financial statements is contained in the letter of engagement.

6   A,C,F

   A profit-related scheme means that directors have the incentive to overstate profit and hence the accounts are susceptible to material fraud/error. Therefore inherent risk is higher than normal. A cash-based business is more inherently risky than a non-cash-based business, as cash is susceptible by its nature to theft and omission. Where balances in the financial statements have straightforward financial accounting requirements, the susceptibility to material error or misinterpretation is reduced.

7   A,C,F

   Option A is correct as the concept of materiality does not exist in a void, but depends on the context of the omission or misstatement. Option C is correct as materiality acts as a form of guidance in the amount of work required to be performed, and so when planning audit procedures. It is also made reference to in evaluating discovered misstatements (both individual misstatements and in aggregate). Option F is correct as materiality is not a fixed % of profits or other measure but depends on the audit risks faced for the particular client. Further, materiality is not only measured quantitatively but also qualitatively.

8   A,D Both the examples increase the susceptibility of the accounts to material fraud and error. The fact the organisation is seeking to raise finance for a new venture represents a risk at the company level, whereas the estimates present a risk at the individual account level where those estimates are found.

9   B,F High staff turnover increases the risk that the internal controls in place will not be effective. The use of samples in testing, represents a sampling risk: that the sample tested will not represent the population as a whole. Sampling risk is part of detection risk.

10   A,D,E

   Warrants further testing – both the balance in the Cost of Sales account and the annual decrease of 7% are significant and therefore further work is required to explain the movement in the gross margin.

   No further testing – the balance of repairs and renewals and the year on year decrease of 4% is not significant (immaterial).

   Warrants further testing – although an increase of 2% is not significant, the balance in the advertising account is material and so further testing to analytical procedures is warranted.

11 A,B Options C and D are incorrect as tests of details and review of events after the date of the financial statements are normally performed after the initial planning stage of the audit.

12 C Analytical procedures help identify material monetary errors in the financial statements (which could be due to changes in account balances or key ratios as a result of mispostings, misclassification errors or under/overstatements). The other techniques are all concerned with systems assessment or testing of controls.

13 A,D,E

Option A is correct as materiality needs to be calculated at the audit planning stage to provide a guide as to the extent of audit procedures required. Option D is correct as materiality can be revised during the course of the audit, as the assessment of audit risk changes. With regards to option E, the materiality level set will have an impact on the audit opinion as the existence of material unadjusted errors and misstatements will lead to a qualified audit opinion.

14 B,D The existence of management override increases control risk as controls may be ignored leading to an increased risk of material fraud or error. Profit related pay may motivate the directors to distort the financial information, so constituting an inherent risk.

15 B,C,E

Options A and D are incorrect as sample sizes and inexperienced audit staff will affect detection risk.

16 B,C If detection risk is low this means that the auditor must have a higher expectation of identifying errors and misstatements. Materiality is lower as the financial statements are more sensitive and sample sizes are increased so that more work is performed.

17 B,F Substantive procedures only – A new client with few employees implies a lack of segregation of duties and hence high control risk. Therefore reliance should not be placed on the internal control system. Audit evidence should be gathered using substantive procedures.

A mix of tests of control and substantive procedures may be used for the audit of a long-standing client with a sophisticated IT system and an internal audit department as it will be possible to rely on internal controls and then perform reduced substantive procedures.

18 B,D If sales prices are cut but costs remain the same gross profit margins will fall. If the company sells a greater proportion of goods with a lower margin than in previous years the overall margin will be reduced. Increased levels of sales (and therefore lower closing inventory) will not affect gross profit margins provided selling prices are maintained. Interest expense is not deducted in arriving at gross profit, therefore it can have no effect on gross profit margins.

19 A,C,F

With a recent listing on the stock exchange and high profit expectations, inherent risk is higher than normal as accounts are more susceptible to material fraud and error. Inventory is by its nature more inherently risky as it is susceptible to theft, omission and misstatement. The fact that the company operates in a slow-moving, stable industry, decreases the susceptibility of the financial statements to material fraud and error.

20 B,C,E

False – materiality can be both quantitative and qualitative.

True – materiality may depend on *either* the nature of an item *or* its monetary amount.

True – materiality is determined by the external auditor and he will use his professional judgment in setting a level of materiality which best addresses the audit risk.

21 B,D Control – few employees indicates limited segregation of duties, which is a control deficiency.

Inherent – a fast-moving, high-tech environment presents inherent risks both at the company level but also at individual account levels (eg inventory).

22 B, D Cash would be decreasing in a situation of overtrading as cash flows out to fund the increases in working capital.

Receivables would be increasing as the company expands without the resources to support the expansion.

23   C   If the entity has purchased a property for cash, this would reduce current assets without any corresponding reduction in current liabilities.

24   D   If the cake shop has a higher level of wastage of inventory than the electrical shop, then this will reduce its cost of sales independently of the mark-up applied. Cost of sales will therefore be high in relation to revenue, so the cake shop's gross margin will be lower.

25   B,D   An unusually large sale would increase receivables and the current ratio.

         If payables are paid out of a positive cash balance then this will reduce both cash (assets) and payables by the same absolute amount. However, since the current ratio is positive (assets are greater than liabilities), the ratio will increase.

1   A   A walk-through test does not provide evidence relating to a specific balance on the financial statements but is used to ensure that the systems operate as the assurance provider believes that it does.

2   A,B   Option C and D are incorrect as evidence from internal sources is not more reliable than evidence created by the assurance provider (in fact, the reverse is true). Furthermore, the statement that photocopies are more reliable than facsimiles is not true as the assurance provider should exercise professional caution with both.

3   A,C,D

Options B and E are incorrect as existence and rights and obligations would be used in respect of a balance, not a class of transactions.

4   A,B,D

Option C is incorrect as positive assurance will be given on an audit assignment, whereas negative assurance is given on a review assignment, reflecting the limited procedures carried out.

5   A,D   Directors refusing to cooperate with the auditor constitute an inability to obtain sufficient appropriate audit evidence – the fact that users discover this has nothing to do with the expectations gap. Shareholders approving the auditor's appointment at a general meeting is a legal obligation of the company.

6   B,F,I

It is only the statutory audit that provides reasonable assurance. The review engagements provide limited assurance. None of the engagements provides absolute assurance.

7   B,F   Option B is correct as where the controls have been assessed as deficient, this means that reliance can not be put on these controls. Option F is correct as where controls have been assessed as strong, this means that they can be relied upon. In this way, tests of controls are carried out coupled with limited substantive procedures.

8   C,E   The Companies Act checklist ensures that all classification issues are addressed. Tracing non-current assets observed back to the non-current asset register ensures that this balance is recorded completely.

9   A,D   Options B and C are incorrect as accuracy and cut-off relate to classes of transactions (ISA 315).

10   C,D   Options A and B are incorrect as cut-off relates to classes of transactions and allocation relates to account balances (ISA 315).

11   A,D,E

Option A is correct as material items must be tested with substantive procedures, although the extent of these procedures will depend on whether reliance can be placed on the related internal controls. Option D is correct as whilst results from tests of controls may affect the extent of substantive procedures they will not eliminate the need for them completely.

12   A,D,E

Observing the opening of the post is a test of control as it is the observation of a control taking place. Calculation of the gross profit margin and comparison with that of the previous accounting period is an analytical procedure (which is, in turn, a substantive procedure). Reviewing for authorisation is also testing that a control has been applied (option E).

13   B,C   As per Companies Act 2006, 'That adequate accounting records have been kept' and 'Directors' remuneration has been disclosed correctly' are reported on by exception.

1   B,F   The process of preparing the financial statements forms part of the information processing system.

Locking the inventory storeroom is a specific control activity.

None of the above relate to the control environment, which refers to the management style and philosophy towards controls.

2   B,D,E

Control risk is lower than normal (ie internal controls are stronger) where the company has an established internal audit function (which strengthens the control environment by monitoring the adequacy and effectiveness of the controls in place) and where the board has a track record of performance review, monitoring and investigating deviations from expected performance. Control risk is higher than normal where purchase invoices are not authorised (control deficiency).

3   B,C,E

Option A is incorrect as all members of an audit committee must be non-executive directors. Option D therefore is also incorrect. The chief internal auditor does not sit on the audit committee, but should ideally report directly to this committee.

4   A,C,D

Option B is not correct as it is the attitude of management and senior staff that will shape the entity's control environment and not that of the ordinary staff.

5   A,D   For the preparation of reconciliations where calculations are involved, the inherent limitation is that these reconciliations are susceptible to human error. Even where duties are segregated, this control can be overridden by the collusion of the parties involved.

6   E   Reporting the process to the auditors is part of the external audit process and not part of the internal risk assessment process.

7   B,C   The information system comprises all the information (be it in hardcopy or electronic form) that flows into the financial statements and does include the whole process of financial statement preparation.

8   C,F   Both are physical controls.

9   B,F   Reconciliations are information processing as they are undertaken to check the completeness and accuracy of information. Having separate clerks recording sales invoices and posting cash receipts in the sales ledger reduces the risk of fraud and error (is therefore a segregation of duties control).

10   A,D,F

Option A is a general control as it supports the effective functioning of application controls. Options D and F are correct as they relate specifically to the processing of individual applications.

11   B   Narrative notes would be the simplest way of recording a straightforward system that was is not subject to a great amount of change annually. It is, however, the least effective way in terms of readily identifying the system in operation and the deficiencies of the system.

12   A,B,D

Option C is not correct as whilst the prior year audit file will be useful, the system may have changed in the intervening period. The company's website is very unlikely to contain details on the internal control system.

13   D   Cyclical reviews of the master files is an application control. The remainder of the options available are general controls.

14   B,D   Options A and C are incorrect as they are control deficiencies, rather than inherent limitations of an internal control system as such.

15   A,B   Appraising the sales ledger constitutes performance review and compiling the trial balance are information processing control activities.

16   B,C   Small companies are less likely to be successful in the implementation of segregation of duties controls due to the limited number of employees available to segregate specific tasks within the various cycles. Given the limited number of staff in small companies and the dominance of management, controls are more likely to be overridden in smaller companies than larger ones.

17   A,E   Training programme for all staff is part of the control environment. Review of actual performance versus budget is a control activity.

18   A,C,F,G

      Option F is the only false item in the question as internal controls should be applied equally to all transactions, whether material or not.

19   A,D,E

      Business risk is of relevance to the auditor as business risks may impact on the financial statements. Management are responsible for identifying and controlling business risks although the auditor will assess business risk as part of the audit.

20   A,B   Options C and D are specific control activities (relating to authorisation).

21   B,C   Information processing, segregation of duties.

      Reasoning as per question 9 of this chapter.

22   A,D,F

      Password protection constitutes a general control. The remaining controls are application controls.

23   C   Procedures for resubmission of rejected data is an application control.

24   B   Narrative notes are more suitable for smaller businesses. Questionnaires do not show relationships and reporting lines as clearly. Although the organisational chart would show the structure of the organisation and general reporting lines, it would not document the system in operation.

25   A,C,F

      A lack of regular reconciliations and management overriding internal controls lead to an increase in control risk (higher than normal). The safeguarding of the physical security of the inventories is a strength which renders control risk lower than normal.

26   A,E   Minimising business risks and complying with laws and regulations are the primary reasons why organisations need effective systems of control. The others may result from that effective internal control system.

27   A,C,E

      Authorisation of transactions, custody or handling of assets and recording of transactions are the three functions which should ideally be separated such that no-one person can initiate the transaction, record that transaction in the accounting records and have custody of assets which arise from that transaction. For fraud to take place, with such segregation of duties, there would have to be significant collusion. Preparing financial statements is a function which follows from the recording of transactions and effective budgetary control can only take place once there is confidence on the integrity of data coming from effective internal control systems.

28   B   An audit committee is made up of non-executive directors only.

29　A,F　The entity's organisational structure is part of the entity's control environment. Monitoring of controls involves a review of the effectiveness of controls and whether they need improving – hence a review by management of monthly bank reconciliations is part of that monitoring system.

30　A,D　Authorisation showing that the accountant has reviewed the reconciliation.

Performance review includes reviews and analyses of actual performance against budgets (as here), forecasts and prior period performance.

31　C　Application controls apply to the processing of individual applications (eg sales, purchases, inventory), hence authorisation of data for input (say of purchase orders) is the application control. The remaining options are general controls, which relate to many applications and support the operation of the whole IT environment.

32　B,E　User selection of passwords and displaying the password on screen would reduce password effectiveness. The existence of frequent changes of passwords, automatic disconnection after failed attempts and disciplinary offences if passwords are revealed would all *increase* password effectiveness.

Chapter 6: Revenue system

1   A,B,D

Option C is not correct as it is a benefit to the company if its customers do not take the full credit period and pay sooner. This would be a risk in the purchases system as it would benefit the company to take the full credit period extended to it by its suppliers.

2   A,D   Authorisations of credit terms to customers and checking the ageing of current receivables ledger balance prior to accepting orders in order to assess the creditworthiness and history of payments. Options B and C are not correct as they are procedures that take place after the customer has made the purchase.

3   A,B,D

Option C, investigation of differences between till records and cash collected, is not a preventative control activity but a detective activity ie it happens after the fact.

4   A,D,F

Option D applies as there is no link between despatch and invoice (goods could be invoiced without being despatched), and there is no link between order and despatch (orders may not be fulfilled). Option F is correct as reception staff are unconnected with any of the departments with whom customers might have a query – ordering, warehouse or accounts.

5   A,C   The duties of authorisation, recording and custody of assets should be segregated

6   B,D   If invoices are matched to orders but not warehouse records, invoices may be raised in error. If receivables statements are not sent to customers, customers may not pay promptly.

7   C,D   If overdue accounts are not followed up, debts might be included on the receivables ledger that are not collectable. Where invoices are not in numerical sequence, invoiced sales might not be properly recorded.

8   A,D   If credit notes are valid then the related invoice is cancelled. Goods received are part of the purchases system. As such, options B and C are not risks associated with the sales system.

9   C   Despatch notes are evidence of goods delivered. If there are sales invoices for each of these all sales will be invoiced. Options A and B are incorrect as they relate to the completeness of sales orders and ensure that all orders are subsequently despatched respectively. Option D is also incorrect as requiring customers to sign for goods confirms delivery only.

10   A,D,E

In process 2 there is insufficient segregation of duties. The same individual should not be responsible for processing invoices, posting cash and performing the control account reconciliation.

11   B,F   If despatch notes are not pre-numbered they may be lost and therefore no invoice raised. If customers do not evidence receipt of goods disputes may arise leading to slow payment.

12   A,D   Correct invoicing is an objective of the invoicing stage of the sales system. Cut-off affects the recording stage of the sales cycle.

13 A,D,E

Strength – that orders placed by telephone, once credit checked, are entered into the system is a strength as it ensures the prompt recording of an order. Also the customer is checked for creditworthiness prior to the order being generated – indicating that the company is protecting itself from loss.

Deficiency – the order should only be accepted once it has been confirmed that the goods ordered are available. The invoice should be generated once it is confirmed that the goods have reached the customer (as evidenced by the customer signing the dispatch note).

Strength – a copy of any dispatch notes with incomplete orders filed and reviewed daily will ensure that orders are filled at a later date.

1 B,F Analysis of actual performance against budget is performance review. Checking numerical sequences helps ensure completeness of records.

2 A,E Option B is incorrect as does not relate to the goods inwards stage of the purchase system. Option C is also incorrect as the question refers to goods and not services. The checking of invoices to orders will reduce the risk of accepting invoices for goods or services which were not ordered.

3 B,C,E

   Deficiency – there is no authorisation of payment orders.
   Strength – company only recognises liability for services received.
   Strength – payments authorised.

4 A,B The answer is not C as inappropriate orders could still be made with authorised suppliers. The answer is not D as once inappropriate orders have been authorised, matching the order with the invoice will not **prevent** that act having taken place.

5 C Jack Frost and Tiny Tim should requisition materials as production needs dictate, but orders should be placed (and by implication authorised) by the purchasing department. The managing director would not be involved in authorising normal purchasing transactions in a company with a purchasing department. Someone other than the production department leaders should authorise purchases.

6 A As it is company policy to record goods only if accepted then a comparison of invoices with goods received records would identify if the goods had not been accepted - as there is no goods received record, the goods must have been faulty (or rejected for some other reason). This would then prevent the invoice from being processed.

7 C,E Checking arithmetical accuracy is an information processing control. Physical security measures should reduce risk of theft.

8 C,D Where goods received notes are not matched to purchase invoices, goods may have been received and not invoiced or where invoices not matched to goods received notes invoices could be posted without having received goods leading to a misstatement of liabilities. Control account reconciliations help to identify posting errors. Options A and B are control deficiencies that do not result directly in the misstatement of liabilities.

9 B,D Purchase of goods from unauthorised suppliers is likely to lead to inferior goods being purchased. By having access to the payables master file, purchase ledger clerks are in a position to create fictitious suppliers and so then enable payments to them.

1   B   It is the temporary staff's work schedules that document the hours worked. As such they require control to ensure that it is only the hours authorised that are subsequently paid.

2   A,B,D

Option C is not correct as it does not relate directly to the employees' payments but to their tax deductions.

3   B,C,E

With regards to option B, clocking in and out of work ensures correct recording of the hours clocked in and out, but has no bearing on the rate of pay.

4   A,C   Both cases lead to the possibility that employees are paid the wrong amounts.

5   A,C,E

All three processes represent strengths. Process 1 involves physical security as a control. Process 2 has elements of performance review and authorisation. Process 3 is also a strength as an authorisation control features.

6   C,D   Options A and B are not correct as authorisation of overtime ensures that the correct number of hours are paid for and reperformance of payroll calculations ensures the accuracy of the deductions etc.

7   B,C   Unauthorised amendments could result in the creation of bogus employees or overpayment of existing employees. Personnel records contain details of pay rates. If these are not kept up to date standing data in the payroll system may also be invalid. Options A and D would not lead to misstatement in the financial statements.

8   A,C,F

Process 3 is false (option F) as whilst the risk of errors are reduced in a computerised payroll system, a sample of calculations should still be checked. This may also bring to light errors with standing data and input.

9   B   In order to prevent this from happening, the key is that fictitious employees never make it onto the payroll. The financial controller is concerned that an employee from the accounts department, who has the right to access the payroll system, might be so unscrupulous as to add a fictitious employee and gain access to the wages.

- Payroll standing data periodically printed out and checked on a line-by-line basis to independently held employee details – this will *detect* fictitious employees added but will not *prevent* fictitious employees from being added.

- Use of hierarchical passwords over standing data files – this will allow the company to restrict access to standing data files to a responsible official, yet still allow other employees to process the wages. This means that an unscrupulous employee *cannot* access the part of the system where new employees would be added and hence will prevent the fraud. This is therefore the correct answer.

- Pre-authorisation of all amendments to payroll standing data by an independent official – an unscrupulous employee will not ask for authorisation – he will simply add the fictitious details if the system allows him to do this.

- Supervision of the wages payout by an independent official – again, this might detect dummy employees but would be unlikely to prevent the fraud.

10   B,D   Access controls and encryption of data will reduce the risk of unauthorised disclosure. Exception reporting and an independent review of the payroll, would help identify unauthorised changes to payroll information. Back-up procedures would help in the protection of company data.

Assurance: Answer Bank

Chapter 9: Internal audit

1 A,B Authorising unusual transactions and developing internal control systems are part of the accounting function in an entity. In order for the internal audit function to operate objectively and independently, it should not be involved in these activities.

2 A,C Options B and D are not correct as they are too operational and would compromise internal audit's monitoring role.

3 B,C,D

Option A is not correct as it is the external auditors who have the legal duty to carry out the statutory audit. It is, however, usually encouraged that there is some co-operation between the internal and external auditors where this is possible.

4 B,C,E

Having an internal audit function is not a requirement of the UK Corporate Governance Code but the need for directors to review the need for one annually is. The other statements are both true.

5 B, D, F

All of the statements are false. Because independence is a concern, internal audit report to the board of directors or the audit committee. The UK Corporate Governance Code does not require listed companies to have an internal audit function per se, but requires companies to consider the need for one annually, in order to maintain an adequate system of internal controls. Internal audit uses both testing of internal controls and substantive testing, as appropriate to the task in hand.

6 B,C Secondment to the financial controller role and being involved in the identification of risks should not be carried out by the internal auditor. This is because these roles are operational and would compromise the ability of internal audit to provide a monitoring role. The risk assessment should be undertaken by the risk assessment committee or whomever is responsible for risk assessment.

7 B,D External auditors are responsible for carrying out the statutory audit. Internal auditors are responsible for the monitoring of internal controls. External auditors, as part of their external audit, will not *monitor* internal controls but must at least ascertain the controls in place and document them. They may then choose to test them for purposes of reliance.

8 D Expressing an opinion on the truth and fairness of the financial statements is done by the external auditor only.

9 B An operational audit is just one type of work carried out by the internal auditor. Other audit work might include, for example, investigation into a suspected fraud. Therefore the term does not apply to all internal audit work.

10 A,C Options B and D are incorrect as external auditors report to the shareholders and, although internal auditors will normally provide information to the external auditors, they do not formally report to them.

11 A,B,D

The external auditor may identify efficiency issues during the course of the statutory audit but audit work is not specifically planned with this objective.

12 A,C,D

Internal audit should not have operational responsibilities so should not authorise transactions or routinely prepare bank reconciliations.

Assurance: Answer Bank

1   A   Confirming the terms of the engagement is done in the engagement letter and does not constitute a reason for assurance providers to record their work.

2   A,C,D

The answer is not option B as the details relating to the planning of the work will be included in the planning memorandum. The answer is not option E as the initials of the person supervising the work are not necessary, but the reviewer would initial the working paper. The supervisor and the reviewer might be the same person, but not necessarily.

3   A,D   Options B, C and E will be kept on the current year audit file.

4   A,C   Option B is incorrect as the ICAEW requires all firms should keep all audit working papers for at least six years from the end of the accounting period to which they relate, so more than the current and previous year will be kept.

Option D is incorrect as working papers belong to the assurance provider so this decision does not belong to the client.

5   A,D,E

The second statement is not valid as documenting fieldwork is a *professional* and not a legal requirement. The other two statements are valid.

6   B,D,G

The engagement letter will be held on the permanent audit file. The audit plan and manager review notes will be on the current file only.

7   B,C,D

Details of the history of the client's business and lease agreements would be held on the permanent audit file.

8   A,C,F

Working papers belong to the auditor and should be stored securely by the auditor in locked premises. Although ISA 230 requires documentation to be kept for a minimum of five years from the date of the auditor's report, the ICAEW requires Registered Auditors to keep all audit working papers required by auditing standards for a period of at least six years from the end of the accounting period to which they relate.

9   A,D,E

The second statement is not valid as there is no direct correlation between the number of working papers produced and the audit fee charged. The other two statements are valid.

10   B,C,E

Not valid – fieldwork documentation does not assist in establishing the audit strategy.

Valid – fieldwork documentation assists in an effective review process.

Valid – the fieldwork documentation provides a record of evidence gathered.

11   B,D,E

The permanent audit file contains documents of ongoing relevance, whereas the current audit file contains documents and working papers that relate directly to the audit of the current year end.

12   A,B,D

Option C is not correct as computerised audit processes cannot replace the exercise of judgement by the auditor.

13 C Six years from the end of the accounting period to which they relate is the ICAEW requirement.

14 C The auditor must ensure the safe custody of audit documentation for at least six years from the end of the accounting period to which it relates.

1   B,D   Inspection of assets does not confirm rights and obligations as the asset might be possessed wrongfully or leased and inspection will not show that. Observation gives only weak evidence of the matter being observed and only at the moment the matter was being observed, not the next time it is done, unobserved.

2   A,B,C

Option D is not correct as test data, as opposed to audit software, is used to test controls over processing.

3   A,C   Whilst analytical procedures must be used at the risk assessment and overall review stages, they need not be used as substantive procedures as tests of details and other procedures may be more appropriate. Although it may be advisable for analytical procedures to be carried out by senior level assurance staff, this is not a requirement of ISA 520.

4   A,B,C

Option D is not correct as the assurance provider may use information that has been internally generated at the entity, provided he is satisfied that information has been properly prepared.

5   D   Recalculating the interest accrued on the basis of outstanding amount, interest rate and period to which it relates would be the most appropriate for verification of the interest accrued on borrowings. Confirming the interest rate with the lender would not verify the total interest accrued balance (as the interest rate is only one component of the calculation) nor would vouching the interest payment (as interest paid is not the same as interest accrued). Testing the internal controls over cash payments would not lead to direct verification of the interest accrued.

6   A,D   When testing for *over*statement (ie seeking to discover errors), the assurance provider will test items from the accounting records to the supporting documents. When testing for *under*statement (ie seeking to discover omissions), the assurance provider will select items from outside the accounting records and trace to the records.

7   B,D   Testing 100% of items in a population and testing all items with a certain characteristic is not sampling, as in the former case the whole population is tested, and in the latter case the 'sample' is not representative of the whole population.

8   C,D   The time available to complete the test and the skill of the team member assigned to carry out the test will not affect the number of items to be tested, whereas risk assessment and expected misstatement will.

9   A,B,E

Sequence sampling would more commonly be used in testing controls. Haphazard selection should not be used when the assurance provider is using statistical sampling.

10   A, E   A misposting between customer accounts and a timing difference between customer records and client records are errors which would not generally be extrapolated against the total value of the population.

11   C,D,H

Documents and other pieces of evidence are inspected. Processes are observed. External confirmations involve seeking evidence from a third party.

12   A,C,F

Audit software makes use of the *assurance provider's* own specialised software. It can extract and analyse information from the client's system. Test data is used to test controls by inputting data which should activate a control and checking that it does so.

13   D   Inspection of a sales invoices produced by the client would constitute the least persuasive
           method of gathering evidence as it is the least reliable of all the options. The supplier's invoice
           is more reliable as it comes from a third party and reperformance of calculations and
           reconciliations is also more reliable as this evidence is generated by the assurance
           provider/reporting accountant.

14   A,C,F

           For *tests of details*:

           When the required confidence level increases the sample size increases (ie the auditor needs
           to do more work to be more confident).

           When the assessed risk of material misstatement for a balance is increased, the sample size
           increases (ie more work is needed for higher risk balances).

           Stratifying the population decreases the sample size (as testing is more efficient).

15   B,F,H

           For *tests of controls*:

           An increase in tolerable misstatement will cause a decrease in sample size as an increase in the
           amount of 'acceptable misstatements' (or audit risk acceptable) will reduce the extent of the
           work necessary to be performed (as there is a corresponding acceptable increase in detection
           risk).

           An increase in the population will have a negligible effect on sample size as it is not a factor
           that determines the sample size.

           A decrease in the auditor's required confidence level will lead to a decrease in sample size.

16   B,D Per ISA 530 regarding factors influencing sample sizes for tests of controls:

           An increase in the number of sampling units will have a negligible effect on the sample size.

           A decrease in the tolerable misstatement will increase sample size.

17   B,C,F

           Physical examination of property, plant and equipment confirms existence (it may belong to a
           third party). The reliability of inquiry depends on who is providing the information. A third
           party eg a bank would normally be a reliable source.

18   B,C,E

           A sales invoice is less reliable than a purchase invoice as it is internally generated. Original
           documents are more reliable than copies. A bank statement is more reliable than a cash book
           as it is generated by a third party.

19   B,C,F

           The weakness of observation of a procedure is that the conclusion drawn as a result only
           applies to the system at the time the observation took place – hence it is limited to the point
           in time it takes place.

           The usefulness of analytical review is limited by the underlying accounting system which
           generates the balances under review.

           A respondent will agree to an overstated balance if that is direct confirmation in respect of a
           payables balance (he would disagree if the amount he owed – ie a receivables balance – were
           overstated).

20   A,D,E

           Per ISA 315, analytical procedures *must* be used at the risk assessment stage of an audit. Per
           ISA 520 they *must* also be used at the overall review stages of an audit and *may* be used as a
           substantive procedure.

21   B,D If budgets are not realistic they will not provide a reasonable basis for comparison with actual.
           Deficiencies in internal controls reduce the reliability of the basic accounting information
           which will be used in the analytical procedures.

22 A,C Tests for understatement (ie omission) cannot start from the source being tested for understatement/omission. They must start from some other source and trace through to the accounting records, to prove that nothing has been omitted (ie the entity's transactions or balances are not understated).

23 A,B,C

Option D is not correct as tolerable misstatement is related to the auditor's judgement about materiality.

24 A,D,E

An increase in the auditor's assessment of the risk of material misstatement would cause the sample size to increase as an increase in audit risk can only be addressed and reduced by an increase in the work carried out.

An increase in the use of analytical procedures to test the same assertion would decrease the sample size, so that the area is not over-audited.

An increase in the expected misstatements would lead to an increase in the sample size.

25 B,C,F

The auditor's main concern in testing assets is that they might be overstated whereas he will be concerned that liabilities might be understated. Communicating with the company's legal advisers about outstanding legal claims is testing for understatement in liabilities. Reviewing the aged inventory analysis is testing for overstatement in the valuation of inventories, as the existence of old/obsolete inventory may require a write-down to net realisable value. Performing the calculation on the warranty provision and then comparing that figure with the balance stated, is testing a liability and therefore testing for understatement.

26 B,C,F

Test data is used to test controls. Audit software (not test data) can be used to assist in the calculation of ratios.

27 A The misstatement that the auditor expects to be present in the population = expected misstatement. Control deviations, when performing tests of control, or misstatements, when performing substantive procedures = misstatement. The maximum error in the population that the auditor would be willing to accept = tolerable misstatement.

28 A,E Systematic selection involves selecting items using a constant interval between selections, the first interval having a random start.

29 B,C,E

Positive confirmations may request that the respondent provides the balance owing as opposed to simply confirming the balance stated. A sample taken from a list of receivables is more effective than for payables, as in this way testing the balance for overstatement is carried out directly. For payables, the auditor's key concern is that of understatement and testing a sample from the payables listed will not test understatement. A positive confirmation is more reliable than a negative confirmation as in the first case, a response is always sought.

Assurance: Answer Bank

1   A,B,C

    Option D is not correct as the level of materiality used during the audit is the responsibility of the auditors.

2   C,D Auditors may only obtain written representations to support other audit evidence (ISA 580 paragraph 13).

    Where evidence is missing due to a fire, this is not a matter to obtain a written representation on but is an inability to obtain sufficient appropriate audit evidence.

3   A,D,F

    Statement 2 is false as this is an inability to obtain sufficient appropriate audit evidence. Statement 3 is also false because if written representations are inconsistent with other audit evidence, the auditor shall perform audit procedures to attempt to resolve the matter. If the matter remains unresolved, the auditor shall reconsider the assessment of management.

4   A,D,F

    Specific written representations may include confirmation from management that accounting policies selected are appropriate, but this is not compulsory.

    Auditors may only obtain written representations to support other audit evidence (ISA 580 paragraph 13).

5   A,C The other two options would not be valid circumstances in which to seek written representations. If information normally expected to be available is unavailable, this would indicate an inability to obtain sufficient appropriate audit evidence. The fact that an alternative audit procedure is time-consuming is not a reason to seek a written representation – a written representation cannot act as a substitute for other evidence which is expected to exist.

6   A,D The auditor should be able to obtain sufficient alternative evidence regarding the existence of plant and equipment and reconciling items on the cash account.

7   B,C,E

    Written representation letters are required on an annual basis so that representations are valid for each specific audit. They should be dated before (although not much before) the auditor's report as they form part of the audit evidence on which the auditor is relying to reach his opinion. The written representation letter must include a list of all uncorrected misstatements as per ISA 450. It shall also include a statement that the directors believe the total of *uncorrected* misstatements to be immaterial to the financial statements as a whole.

8   B,C,F

    It is usually only of senior management that auditors request written representations as they are responsible for matters of judgment, cooperating with the auditors etc.

    Written representations cannot be used as a substitute for other evidence that is expected to be available.

9   A,C Acknowledgement that management has fulfilled its responsibility for the preparation of the financial statements and acknowledgement by management of its belief that the aggregate of uncorrected misstatements are immaterial to the financial statements are the two purposes of the written representation letter from the list provided.

    Where other evidence is available on a matter, the written representation letter does not serve to provide evidence. Management's confirmation of the scope of the work to be carried out is included in an engagement letter.

1   A,B,C

The rights and obligations assertion means that the entity holds or controls the rights to assets. Although vehicle registration documents show registered keeper, not owner, the keeper is likely to have control of the asset. Both title deeds and purchase invoices give evidence of ownership (which gives control). Sales invoices give evidence of no longer having ownership of something and do not therefore *support* the rights and obligations assertion.

2   D   Cut-off is a financial statement assertion that affects classes of transactions, not account balances.

3   A,B,C

Inventory has not been disclosed properly in the financial statements constitutes the lowest risk, as the disclosure requirements in relation to inventory are not onerous. In contrast, inventory is often easy to conceal or omit from records or count wrongly, and, as it usually consists of a large number of items, valuation can be tricky also.

4   B,C   Post year-end sales invoices and orders. The controls over counting relate to existence, not valuation. A post year-end sales price list gives evidence of management intention in relation to inventory, but not evidence of the price that customers are genuinely prepared to pay (in the way that invoices and orders do).

5   B   The fact that a positive confirmation requires the customer to reply to confirm or deny the balance (or to reply giving the balance) is the reason why this method is generally preferred in preference to a negative confirmation. This is because a negative confirmation *only* requires a reply if the balance is not agreed – thereby giving poorer quality evidence as if there is no reply the auditor cannot be sure that the customer has not just ignored the letter (or whether he has even received it). The answer is not option A as negative confirmations are also carried out in the auditor's name. Option C describes a negative confirmation and so is not correct. Option D does not apply to any type of confirmation.

6   B,C   Direct confirmations with customers and review of cash paid after date are most appropriate as these provide *independent* confirmation of the year-end trade receivables balance, whereas the receivables ledger and sales invoices are part of the client's own records.

7   C   Inspection of the bank letter gives the most reliable evidence as this is received by the auditor directly from the bank. Bank statements have been sent via the client, so there is scope for them to have been tampered with in some way. Bank reconciliations and the cash book are client-generated documents and are, therefore, less reliable.

8   A,D   The auditor should count an individual cash float which is material because he should test all material items. He should also count immaterial cash floats where he suspects that a fraud has been committed as although the individual floats are immaterial, the overall impact of such a fraud could be material to the financial statements if repeated over time.

9   A   Completeness (ie understatement), as liabilities are generally tested for understatement, as they are more likely to be understated than overstated. Existence (overstatement) is a higher risk assertion for assets, as opposed to liabilities. Disclosure is generally a less risky assertion in any case. Accuracy applies to transactions and not account balances.

10   B,C,D

Although a payables circularisation does provide third party evidence, it is unnecessary on those grounds alone, because supplier statements provide third party evidence as well. Therefore a payables circularisation will only be needed where there is some problem, such as those described in options B, C and D.

11 B,C Option B is correct – that sales constitute a high volume of similar transactions and are hence suitable to controls testing. Regarding option C – where controls are expected to be strong, ISA 330 requires that the auditors test them so this is also correct. Option A cannot be used as a reason for testing internal controls over sales – however many transactions there are, if controls appear to be deficient, then those transactions will need to be subjected to tests of detail. Option D is incorrect as where there is a high risk of misstatement, substantive procedures should be used.

12 B,C,D

Applying analytical procedures to the operating margin which contains the effect of *all* expenses, not just purchases, will not provide direct evidence as to the accuracy of purchases.

13 C,D Extending the sample of assets inspected will test if the misstatement found to date is an anomaly or represents a larger misstatement.

Vouching the revalued building to a valuer's report is sufficient to enable a conclusion to be drawn.

14 C,E For the misstatement in cut-off, the sample should be extended to measure the full extent of the cut-off misstatement.

Missing supplier statements (which should make the auditor suspicious) should be referred to a senior colleague, so that this is investigated and alternative procedures designed if necessary.

15 B,D Both disagreements are due to timing differences and hence do not constitute misstatements in the accuracy of total trade receivables.

16 B,C The first statement represents a test of control over inventory counting procedures and therefore the completeness or existence of the quantity of inventory. It is not a test of valuation. Checking inventory items against sales invoices tests for NRV and hence valuation of the inventory.

17 A,D,E

The current account balance should be tested as it is over the materiality threshold.

The petty cash float is not material and hence need not be tested.

The special directors' cash account should be tested whatever its monetary value. Strict materiality thresholds do not apply to directors' emoluments which need to be disclosed whatever their amount. In any case the auditor needs to ascertain what this balance represents.

18 A,C,F

Analytical procedures are useful for detecting incomplete figures (ie the auditor can calculate what figure he expects and then compare the actual to it).

Tracing from GRNs to the payables ledger and financial statements proves the completeness of purchases/payables (ie that all goods received have been recorded as purchase/payables).

Tracing a sample of entries on the payroll to HR records does not test completeness as the direction of testing is from the payroll balance to the source documentation.

19 B,D Only existence and rights and obligations are assertions about account balances. Occurrence, classification and accuracy are assertions in respect of classes of transactions and events for the period.

20 C Testing for omissions is the same as testing for completeness (ie nothing has been omitted from the register means the same as saying the register is complete).

21 A,C Physical inspection and confirmation of calculations provide evidence of existence and valuation respectively as opposed to rights and obligations.

The rights and obligations assertion means that the entity holds or controls the rights to assets. Although registration documents show registered keeper, not owner, the keeper is likely to have control of the asset. Purchase invoices give evidence of ownership (which gives control).

22 C,E The cut-off assertion is affected by including inventory sold in inventory at the end of the period (ie cut-off is incorrect). Where damaged items have not been written down to NRV, then the valuation assertion is directly affected (ie inventory is incorrectly valued).

23 A,E The completeness assertion is affected by the omission of inventory items (ie inventory is not complete).

The valuation assertion is affected by miscalculations of cost and the not writing down of damaged items (ie inventory is incorrectly valued).

24 B,D,E

The inventory count should involve personnel who are independent of the warehouse staff. Count sheets should be completed in pen so that there is a permanent record. By having two teams of counters involved in the inventory count, there is a check within the inventory counting process that the count is being carried out correctly.

25 A,D,E

All inventory lines must be counted at least once per year, not once per month.

26 A,C,D

An increase in selling price *increases* net realisable value. Trade discounts from suppliers *reduce* cost.

27 A,C Valuation is not supported as we have no evidence that these receivables intend to pay. Completeness is not supported as it is the list of receivables provided by the client that is subject to direct confirmation (ie the test is for existence and ownership (= rights and obligations) from that list). Occurrence is a financial statement assertion that affects classes of transactions and not account balances.

28 A,C,F,H

The negative method of direct confirmation of receivables (ie only receiving responses by exception) *could* be used when a substantial amount of misstatements is not expected and there is no need to believe that respondents will disregard these requests. In other circumstances the positive method should be used.

29 B Whereas the procedures described in A, C and D are helpful with respect to the valuation assertion, subsequent receipt of cash confirms absolutely that the balance was recoverable at the year end.

30 B,C If the auditor cannot rely on the internal controls in place, because they are deficient, he will need to rely completely on substantive procedures. Client A, a newly formed company without a financial controller, will be unlikely to have effective internal controls therefore the auditor will need to rely completely on substantive procedures. Client B is an established company with apparent controls in place so the auditor should be able to test and rely on those controls.

31 A,C,F

Test of control – that the instructions are likely to lead to an accurate count.

Test of control – that despatch procedures are being properly followed.

Substantive procedure – remembering that substantive procedures include analytical procedures, which is what this describes.

32 B,F Recalculation consists of checking the mathematical accuracy of documents or records, therefore casting the list of year-end receivables is a recalculation procedure.

Reperformance is the auditor's independent execution of procedures or controls which were originally performed as part of the entity's internal control, therefore using CAATs to check the ageing of the year-end list of aged receivables is a reperformance of that ageing analysis, which is itself a control over the recoverability of receivables.

33   B,C,E

False – a positive confirmation may take two forms: requesting a response indicating whether they agree or disagree with the information provided, or requesting the recipient to state the amount owed by/to them.

True – receivables are tested for overstatement therefore it is acceptable to select the sample from the client's list of balances. The direct confirmation would be likely to elicit a response (even if negative confirmation is used) if the balance is indeed overstated. However, payables are tested for understatement and the auditor is looking for balances which are not on the client's list, but should be. Therefore this sample should be drawn from a list of all possible payables, not from the client's list, which may already be understated.

True – with a positive confirmation, a response is expected whether there is agreement or disagreement. With a negative confirmation, there is an element of uncertainty as to the reasons for non-response. Hence the former is ordinarily more reliable than the latter.

34   C   Completeness – a sequence check will highlight missing documents which may indicate unrecorded transactions – ie test the completeness of sales.

35   C   Obtaining direct confirmation of the bank balance from the client's bank will confirm the existence of the cash at bank with a third party (ie the bank).

36   B,D   Not misstatement – this disagreement stems from a timing difference and, as such, does not indicate a misstatement in the receivables balance.

Not misstatement – this disagreement stems from a misposting which does not affect the total receivables balance in the financial statements.

37   A,F   Overstatement – the amount is an asset so we test primarily for overstatement. The amount owed is considered irrespective of the materiality threshold due to the nature of the item (director loan).

Not test – the amount is below the materiality threshold. The likelihood of material fraud or misstatement within the balance is very low.

38   C   Actual inventory levels at branches are higher than book inventory – ie there must be unrecorded goods inwards. Only unrecorded branch requisitions (goods coming in from head office) would explain this. All the others would lean to book inventory higher than actual inventory.

39   A,F,H

No misstatements are found therefore the appropriate action would be to draw a conclusion.

An arithmetic misstatement of £5,000 found would be above the materiality threshold and so the auditor should extend his sample.

A misstatement of £10 found, sanctioned by the FD should lead to the auditor to refer the matter to a senior colleague due to the FD's sanctioning.

40   C   To test for existence the reporting accountant should work from the financial statements to the physical item. However, the financial statements themselves do not contain an analysis of the individual items that make up non-current assets so the reporting accountant will need to select his sample from the non-current asset register (having checked that this record agrees to the financial statements).

1   A,B,C

> There is no legal requirement for ethical codes.

2   B,C   ICAEW qualified auditors acting in the UK are subject to the ICAEW Code and the FRC Ethical Standards for Auditors.

3   A,B,D

> Independence and Courtesy (options C and E) are not fundamental principles of the IFAC Code.

4   C   As per the ICAEW Code of Ethics, the Code applies to its members, employees of member firms and ICAEW students.

5   B,C,E

> The first statement is false as following prescriptive rules of ethical guidance may become a mechanical process without due consideration given to the ethical principles of each case. The other statements are true.

6   A,B,D

> The IAASB issues ISAs, but not ethical guidance (which is issued by IFAC, through the IESBA).

7   B   Although there are some specific 'rules', the majority of ethical guidance is in the form of principles, the spirit of which should be followed by the assurance provider.

8   C,E,I,L

> Both the IFAC Code of Ethics and the FRC Ethical Standards for Auditors identify the following five threats: self-interest, self-review, advocacy, familiarity and intimidation. The FRC Ethical Standards for Auditors also identify the management threat in addition.

9   A,B,D

> Tradition (option C) is not a valid reason why objectivity and independence matter.

10   B,D,F

> A code based on principles does not contain specific rules for auditor compliance.
>
> A rules-based code does not require auditor adherence to a set of principles.
>
> The ICAEW uses a principles-based approach.

1   A,B,C

> Making disclosures to the ICAEW (option D) is no substitute to the other options A, B, C.

2   A,B,D

> Option C is not correct here as a parent of a member of an audit team may own a material financial interest in an audit client – provided they are not a dependant, which would not normally be assumed to be the case.

3   A,C,D

> Option B does not apply as given the staff member does not yet work for the audit client, there is no risk of self-review at this stage.

4   B   Cash It Ltd is a threat as it is implied that an audit team member took advantage of the loan rate mentioned in the audit tendering process.

> Nationally plc is not a threat as it is acceptable for staff to have mortgages on commercial terms with an audit client who is a mortgage provider, especially if it is the leading building society.

5   A   For non-listed companies, there is a presumption of dependence when annual fee income from all services to the client will regularly exceed 15% of gross practice income.

6   A,B,C

> Option D is not correct as it is assistance that is provided as opposed to management or operational decisions being taken.

7   A,B,C

> There is no significant threat to the independence of the audit engagement of Scrabble plc, as the partner had previously rotated off the client six years ago and is allowed to return to the same position after five years.

8   B,C   Doing nothing is not an option available to the ethics partner. It is best to seek to resolve this matter internally by discussing it with the management board of partners whilst at the same time, soliciting advice from the ICAEW to ensure that an acceptable resolution is reached. Seeking the opinion of another ethics partner would probably not be deemed appropriate as the specifics of the case are probably confidential and the ICAEW would be the authority in this area as to the appropriate course of action to be taken.

9   A,D   Prior to seeking legal advice or even resigning (options B and C), Julia should initially try to resolve this issue internally by reporting concerns to the audit committee (which will exist in a listed company) and by obtaining advice from the human resources department at KiwiCorp plc (as to the official internal mechanisms that she can use to make her complaint).

10   A,C,E

> All three cases are examples of the stated threats to auditor independence.

11   A,D   Loesdon Ltd: Self-interest and intimidation threats arise, therefore select self-interest (intimidation is not available as an option). Litten Ltd: Self-interest and intimidation threats arise, therefore select self-interest (intimidation is not available as an option). Management and self-review threats would only arise if the advisory work was accepted.

12   B,E   Othello Ltd: Accept with safeguards (as there are self-interest and self-review threats. There may also be a management threat with regards to the advice provided, so care must be taken not to take management decisions). Desdemona Ltd: Accept with safeguards (despite the time lag, the finance director may have too good a knowledge of the firm's procedures).

13 B,D Per ES5, familiarity and management are the main threats to independence created by the provision of recruitment services. A familiarity threat arises from a close long-standing relationship between the assurance provider and the client (which may start at the point of recruitment). A management threat arises because the assurance provider is acting in a management role. Option A, self-review, is not correct as the assurance provider will not subsequently review the work from the recruitment process. Option C, advocacy, is also incorrect as the assurance provider is not representing the interests of the client in a bid to secure or protect a particular interest.

14 B,F Fussy Ltd: a familiarity threat is possibly present as the prior year audit team may have developed personal relationships with client staff which may threaten their objectivity. Pernickety Ltd: by expressing his dissatisfaction, the finance director is posing an intimidation threat – effectively seeking a different audit opinion or threatening the auditors with replacement.

15 B,D Where there is a high proportion of fee income derived from a particular client (the 5% and 10% rules), if the amount is not prohibitive (the 10% and 15% rules), then safeguards should be put in place. One safeguard would be to discuss the issues with the audit committee, if there is one (which there would be for a major listed company).

Having separate personnel assigned where there are competing clients is the most appropriate safeguard to protect independence.

16 B,E Snowman Ltd: Assuming that this is not a listed company, then provided certain safeguards are applied (such as different teams), the auditor can provide both accounting and auditing services.

Snowball Ltd: Where a client's competitor is also prospectively to be audited by the same auditor, the auditor may accept the appointment with safeguards (such as separate personnel).

17 A,C,D

Both B and E present a self-review threat as opposed to a self-interest threat.

18 B,D,E

A firm should not accept a fee calculated on a contingency basis. Where total fees exceed 15% (10% for a listed entity) of the annual fee income of the firm there is a presumption of dependence and the firm should resign. Where total fees exceed 10% (5% for a listed entity) safeguards should be applied as necessary.

19 C Sam Brown has been a director of Hastle Ltd within the last two years and therefore cannot be used on the audit. James Andersen had the role of office junior and as such was not in a position to exert direct and significant influence over the subject matter of the audit – therefore he can be used on the audit of Hastle Ltd, even though it is only six months' since he resigned. Sally Jones' position, whilst one where she would have been able to exert direct and significant influence over the subject matter of the audit , falls outside the two year period, therefore she could be used on the audit of Morgan Ltd.

20 B Resolving ethical conflicts should be kept in-house where possible.

21 A,D,E

If a partner, a person in a position to influence the outcome of that engagement (eg the audit manager), or an immediate family member of either of these (eg spouse) has a financial interest in a company the firm cannot accept appointment unless the interest is disposed of. As long as Sam Larson is excluded from the audit of Burton Ltd, the firm can accept the appointment.

22 A,F By assigning separate personnel to each assignment the confidentiality of each client and hence the auditor's independence will be protected.

An internal audit role cannot be taken on per ES5 where the audit firm would need to rely on their own work (self-review threat) or where the audit firm would take on part of the role of management (Panama and Co would be responsible for implementing their own recommendations – a management threat). Hence there are no safeguards possible.

23 B,D For non-listed companies, assurance providers can provide accounts preparation assistance provided that adequate safeguards are in place (eg the use of separate teams). Tax advice may be provided but the fee charged cannot be calculated on a contingency basis.

24 A,C,F

Inheriting shares in an audit client immediately creates a financial interest on the part of the auditor.

The audit client providing two free golf lessons to audit staff may create a self-interest threat, as audit staff may be eager to please their client to gain such benefits, than be truly objective in carrying out their audit.

The external auditor providing internal audit services to a client creates a self-review threat, as the external auditor is then likely to review his own work.

25 C Jane should *initially* seek advice from the ICAEW before deciding on her next steps. The general approach to resolving conflicts should be firstly to resolve within the employer *if possible*, then seek advice from the ICAEW, then take legal advice, then resign (perhaps on legal advice, but, in any case, as a last resort).

26 B,D,E

The car loan has been given at a special rate and is likely to be material to the audit manager. All other loans are in the normal course of business on commercial terms.

27 B,C Advocacy threat as the auditor is taking the part of the client in underwriting the client's shares in a flotation.

Self-review threat as the audit firm will be preparing the financial statements and will then review them (though the use of separate teams would reduce this threat).

28 C Management threat – selection of systems should be carried out by management. If the auditor undertakes this role he becomes too closely aligned with management and this threatens his independence.

Self-review threat – the audit firm will audit the system it has implemented.

There are no indications of a familiarity threat, as no indication is given of the length of the relationship nor of any family or close personal relationships between audit firm and client.

29 C NGI is a threat as a personal guarantee appears to have been given by the auditor in favour of the company, in return for the audit should the buy out take place. Hence there is a dependency that threatens the independence of the assurance provider.
NatEast plc is not a threat as the loan to Hammers & Co is modest and in the normal course of business for a major high street bank.

30 A,C,F

Valuations are only prohibited for *non-listed* companies where the item to be valued is material to the financial statements *and* involves a significant degree of subjectivity (for *listed* companies, any material valuation is prohibited). However, safeguards must be implemented to minimise self-review (eg the valuation should be carried out by a different team). Assisting a non-listed company with accounts preparation is acceptable with safeguards to ensure that the role of management is not assumed by the audit firm. No safeguards are possible with the design and implementation of the IT system as the very same system is relied upon for the purposes of the external audit.

31 C Accept Beta Ltd as 12% is below the 15% threshold for private companies. Refuse Alpha plc as 11% is above the 10% threshold for listed companies.

32 A,E Do not accept Titania plc as it is not acceptable to prepare and audit the financial statements of a listed company.

The audit of Puck Ltd can be accepted with safeguards – such as not letting the FD's brother take any part in the audit.

33 A,F At Oberon and Co, the junior can go ahead and perform the work, given the low risk nature of the receivables balance, and the fact that the junior has covered this in his training. The junior is also to join an audit team, where resources for guidance, supervision and review will also be available.

With regards to Lear and Co, the junior should contact ICAEW telephone helpline. Commencing the audit of a client unsupervised, may lead to exposure of both the junior and the firm to risks. In a larger firm the junior could refer to his training partner, but since this is a sole practitioner firm the practitioner himself must also be the training partner.

34 B,D David has no other option in this case but to resign his post and take legal advice. Given that these instructions have come from the board of directors, it would seem fruitless to pursue this issue internally.

35 B,D The FD having a very strong personality may lead to an intimidation threat.

The audit and client team remaining unchanged for many years is likely to lead to a familiarity threat.

36 C An intimidation threat arises because of Mr Black's attitude. There is an advocacy threat if the firm acts in the company's defence. A self-interest threat arises because the firm will be afraid of losing the audit fee.

1   A,C   Options B and D are not the principal reasons for the importance of confidentiality.

2   A,B,D

>   Option C does not apply as accountants may discuss client matters with colleagues in non-public places.

3   A,C,D

>   Option B is not correct as it is not acceptable to disclose confidential information in a bid to secure further audit evidence.

4   B,C,D

>   Where a fraud has been identified, this is usually reported to the client unless the fraud has been carried out by senior management/directors, in which case, great care should be taken in the steps taken.

5   C,D   In the first case, report to the firm's MRLO as the case is suspicious. In the second case, make no external report as there is no public or legal duty to disclose an internal control deficiency.

6   A,C,F

>   In the first case the assurance provider may make disclosure. In case 2, he may make disclosure if the client does not. In the final case, the auditor has a duty to make disclosure as this constitutes money laundering.

7   B   The other options do not apply. Terrorist activities should be reported to the police. Tax evasion should be reported to the Serious Organised Crime Agency (SOCA). Where compliance with the law is required, non-compliance should also be reported.

8   D   The money laundering reporting officer will then decide on the appropriate course of action

9   B,C,F

>   If the audit firm believes that the conflict of interest can be managed through safeguards the firm can continue to act for both parties (option B). The clients involved however, should be informed of the situation (option F).

10   A,C   Encouraging others to buy shares in a company on the basis of information obtained during the course of the audit is known as insider dealing and is a criminal offence. Where audit evidence obtained in the audit of one client affects the audit of another client, procedures must be performed so that the same evidence is obtained from another source.

11   B   In order to avoid giving an incorrect audit report to another client is the only option where permission must first be granted (otherwise the assurance provider will be breaking his duty of confidentiality to that client). For the other options, client permission is not required (and indeed to seek this could be regarded as 'tipping off' the client) but disclosure is necessary by law or the auditor is protected by the court (eg in a negligence claim).

12   D   Report the matter to a designated officer within your firm without the client's permission. Discussing or mentioning the matter with the client would only serve to tip him off about the transactions identified.

ICAEW

REVIEW FORM – ASSURANCE QUESTION BANK

Your ratings, comments and suggestions would be appreciated on the following areas of this Question Bank:

	Very useful	Useful	Not useful
Number of questions/answers	☐	☐	☐
Standard of answers	☐	☐	☐

	Excellent	Good	Adequate	Poor
Overall opinion of this Question Bank	☐	☐	☐	☐

Please add further comments below:

Please return to:

The Learning Team
Learning and Professional Department
ICAEW
Metropolitan House
321 Avebury Boulevard
Milton Keynes
MK9 2FZ
ACAFeedback@icaew.com
www.icaew.com